QUALITY OF LIFE

QUALITY
OF LIFE

How to Get It,
How to Keep It

Shauna Ries, L.C.S.W.,
and
Genna Murphy, L.P.C.

EAGLE BROOK

AN IMPRINT OF
WILLIAM MORROW AND COMPANY, INC.

New York

Published by Eagle Brook
An Imprint of William Morrow and Company, Inc.
1350 Avenue of the Americas, New York, N.Y. 10019

The Twelve Principles of Time Management on pages 33–34 and Fitness
Disguised as Everyday Life on pages 110–111 are reprinted with the
permission of Stresscare Systems, Inc., and Ted Barash.

It is the policy of William Morrow and Company, Inc., and its imprints and
affiliates, recognizing the importance of preserving what has been written,
to print the books we publish on acid-free paper, and we exert our best
efforts to that end.

Library of Congress Cataloging-in-Publication Data

Ries, Shauna.
Quality of life: how to get it, how to keep it
/Shauna Ries & Genna Murphy.—1st ed.
p. cm.
Includes bibliographical references.
ISBN 0-688-16744-6
1. Quality of life.   I. Murphy, Genna.   II. Title
BF637.C5R54   2000
158—dc21   98-49836
CIP

Printed in the United States of America

First Edition

1 2 3 4 5 6 7 8 9 10

BOOK DESIGN BY SUSAN HOOD

www.williammorrow.com

To our clients

In loving memory of

Betty Brady Ries
"Mom"

Virginia Wilkening Wood
"Aunt Ginny"

Do NOT TRY TO SATISFY YOUR VANITY BY TEACHING A GREAT MANY THINGS. AWAKEN PEOPLE'S CURIOSITY. IT IS ENOUGH TO OPEN MINDS; DO NOT OVERLOAD THEM. PUT THERE JUST A SPARK. IF THERE IS SOME GOOD INFLAMMABLE STUFF, IT WILL CATCH FIRE.

ANATOLE FRANCE

Acknowledgments

We wish to thank the following individuals for their help and inspiration over the years:

Our families: Michael James Herrick; Ed Ries; the late Betty Ries; Grace Baron; Tom and Velda Ries and their sons, Eddie and Patrick; Kathy Ries and Merle Krauzer and their children, Christie, Amy, Tom, and Jeff Jackson; and my grandnephews, Alex Wilken, Jared Lieb, and Benjamin Baker.

Drs. John and Charlotte Murphy Jr.; Drs. John and Susan Murphy III and their children, Megan, John IV, and Justin; Dr. Kevin and Charlotte Murphy and their children, Shawn, Shannon, Katie, and Molly; Dr. Brad and Tricia Murphy and their sons, Stephen and Brendan; and Dr. Terry Murphy.

The International Institute of Health and Wellness team: Barry Shapiro, Michael Davidoff, Adena Day Tryon, Amy Kelsall, Mary English, and Dr. Maureen Flory. *Our licensees:* Tom McSherry in Arizona, Dr. Tom Connelly in Washington, D.C., and Pamela King in Florida.

Our friends and colleagues who helped with our book: First and foremost our agent, Linda Konner, and our publisher at Eagle Brook, Joann Davis, and Michelle Shinseki. Our friends and colleagues: Kate Guilford, Barbara Reed, Jan Autry, Marianne McCollum, Jackie Szablewski, Grace Baron, Leslie Vinette, Christi Roseth, Robert Clark, Kim McCullough, J.D., Dirk Biermann, J.D., Dr. Eugene O'Neill, and Dr. Paul Rosch.

Acknowledgments

The teachers who inspired us: Dr. Sue Henry, Dr. Ruth Parsons, Dr. Pam Metz, Steve Litt, L.C.S.W., Susan Pass, L.C.S.W., Dave Blair, L.C.S.W., Dr. Ken Suslak, Dr. Tom Yock, Dr. David Patterson, Dr. Marianne Keatley, Dr. Cynthia Behrman, Dr. Stuart Grover, Dr. Peter Celms, Devi Records, Phil Del Prince, Pat Patterson, Liz Caile, Dee Lover, John Murphy Jr., Charlotte Murphy, Ed Ries, and Betty Brady Ries.

Contents

Contents

Contents

Introduction

———

WAKE UP!

Imagine for a moment you are standing in your kitchen holding a large bullfrog over a pot of boiling water. What do you think this frog would be doing? Most likely he would be thrashing about, trying to spring free from your hand and escape the steamy cauldron below. He is biologically wired for this response and will do whatever he can to escape this sudden danger.

Now imagine you place this same frog in a deep pot of room-temperature water. He may try to climb the sides, but there is no immediate danger and he quickly settles down into the water. You may even place a lily pad or two in the pot just to make it homey. Next, you turn on the heat very slowly so the pot will take a good hour to reach boiling. The frog does not recognize the danger and after about ten minutes begins to stretch out and relax. Another ten minutes pass as the water heats to a mild warmth, and the frog becomes drowsy and more relaxed. Another ten minutes pass, and he falls asleep on the pretty lily pad. The heat continues its slow, surreptitious rise until the frog's internal organs become distressed and his sleep becomes a coma. Ten minutes later, he is dead in the boiling water. He never knew what hit him.

The parable of the boiling frog demonstrates how subtle change can lull humans into a false sense of safety. Like the frog, many of us have become unable to recognize when our lives place us in a slow-heating pot of water. We keep adjusting and adjusting to the heat, until the heat begins to destroy us. Maybe it is a relationship that slowly goes sour, a job that eats away at our passion and aliveness, or drugs or alcohol that lulls us into thinking everything is okay. So we sit in the pot, blow up a floating lounge chair, slather on the sunscreen, and sit back and relax. Pretty soon we are asleep. We never knew what hit us.

This book will help you determine what matters most while showing you how to turn down the heat in your life. As mental health counselors, we wrote *Quality of Life* after discovering that many of our clients were under great stress and unable to cope with it. At the core of this inability to cope, we discovered, clients often feel stuck or trapped. They may entertain ideas of doing something exciting and different yet do not know how to escape. Even if they can feel the temperature rising, many are simply too worn out to try life another way.

You may see yourself in some of the stories we present. You will certainly be reminded of family, friends, and colleagues as you read through the book. They, like many of the clients who walk into our offices, have been in a simmering pot, unable to see the signs until they are seduced into a stupor and the boiling commences. How does this happen? One degree at a time. Slowly, imperceptibly, their lives lose direction and meaning. Their sanity does not vanish overnight. It erodes one particle at a time until they begin behaving in ways they never would have imagined. Perhaps they strike out at loved ones, throw anything and everything into their bodies, explode at the smallest provocation, or rush to destinations they never wanted to reach in the first place.

We began to compile interventions used with our clients over a combined twenty-year period and found commonalities that proved useful and successful. We spent the next two

2

years organizing these materials into a seminar program. We have watched these basic concepts change participants' lives. It worked for them; now let's put it to use for you!

Our book contains many case studies that highlight the issues presented in each chapter. The persons represented in these stories are based on many different clients' stories, family and friends' recollections, and personal experiences woven into fictional characters to protect the confidentiality of real people. Psychotherapy is a completely confidential process between therapist and client. Therefore, any client information we used is well blended with other information to protect clients' identities. Any resemblance to actual persons is unintended.

This book is about turning down the heat, one degree at a time if necessary, and finding ways out of the pot before it boils. It may seem unfair that this world consists of so many pots of slowly heating water. The good news is that every pot presents wonderful possibilities. And so this book is ultimately about waking up to the countless possibilities in your life: possibilities to become more alive, more yourself, more at peace, and more in your passion.

We encourage you to use this book to wake up, shake off the spell of affluence, and give more of yourself to your community. We have organized a plan for accomplishing this that is based on turning down the heat in four areas of your life: (1) time, information, money management, and burnout; (2) negative thinking; (3) poor health and fitness; and (4) troubled relationships. Within each of these four parts resides the nitty-gritty of American life.

In Part 1, we demonstrate how clients present their struggles to manage time, information, and finances. We also focus on the timely issue of burnout and how to recognize its signs and treat it. The last chapter includes a discussion of the benefits of generosity. Turning down the heat on negative thinking is the focus of Part 2, which shows how clients strive to change the way they interpret their world from one of negativity to one of hope and promise.

In the area of health in Part 3, clients struggle with the needs of their bodies concerning nutrition, exercise, relaxation, and self-image. Finally, many clients are engaged in a search for intimate, loving relationships that will sustain them in the most difficult of times. Part 4 discusses relationship issues such as community building, boundaries, assertiveness, couples, and families.

TURNING DOWN THE HEAT

This book will help you evaluate where you are in your life. You will learn how you relate to time, money, and information and how to make changes in these relationships in order to enjoy life more. You will learn to clarify the values that are at the root of your every action and to determine whether your current lifestyle supports these values. You will see how affluence can be an empty dream, how burnout can be conquered, and how generosity can make you a healthier, happier person.

This book is meant as a guide for living more in balance with your natural needs. The ideas and exercises are all suggestions. We recommend that you try as many of them as you like in your own life. Some will be just what you are looking for; some will not fit your unique needs or values. We believe these are some of the best recommendations for changing lifestyles that we have found.

You will understand how to think in ways that support happiness and success. You will learn how to treat your mind and body in ways that give you the energy and good health necessary to live your dreams. You will discover how to create a balanced community that gives you the strength and support to take risks. We assume you are in a pot of hot water somewhere in your life. This book is about turning down the heat in your life. Turning down the heat brings a quality life. A quality life brings happiness. If you're interested in happiness, please . . . read on!

Chapter 1

What Is a Quality Life?

A *quality life* is a state of living in which you are in balance or alignment. This means that what you say aligns with what you think, aligns with what you feel, aligns with how you behave. It is a way of living based on what you value. Athletes may refer to such a state as being "in the zone"; spiritual leaders may speak of this alignment as a state of grace or flow; and psychology refers to it as being congruent or in integrity. Think back to a time when you experienced a state of balance, when everything seemed easy and life required little effort or struggle. Wouldn't you like to create more of this in your life?

We have found that improvement in alignment improves life quality. We believe there are fundamental guiding principles in life that create balance, grace, flow, and integrity. In this chapter, we describe seven principles that underlie the four areas discussed in this book. If you can begin to improve your understanding of and relationship to these seven basic principles, you will experience a vastly improved quality of life.

There are inevitable crises and tragedies in every person's journey. The ideas offered in this chapter and in the entire book are meant to be a compass or guide, not a foolproof map that will lead you to a determined goal. Nobody has a journey unmarked by some manner of tragedy, failure, or personal challenge. However, we believe that when people are closer to balance in most areas of their life, they are better able to handle their unexpected and difficult moments.

SEVEN PRINCIPLES OF A QUALITY LIFE

1. Life is a process; enjoy the journey.
2. It is not as simple as simplifying.
3. Lasting change happens one degree at a time.
4. Every change affects a larger system.
5. Love is more than the Golden Rule.
6. Practice curiosity instead of judgment.
7. Life happens—only you can choose how you see it.

Life is a Process; Enjoy the Journey

Carl Rogers, a leader in the field of self-development, believed that the good life is a direction, not a goal. It is time to let up on the relentless pressure of "working on ourselves" and see that this life is a journey to be enjoyed. When our clients begin to berate themselves for moving too slowly or making mistakes, we use the metaphor of a garden to give them perspective. It is important that they couch their own growth in terms of a living organism. If they start to become impatient, we ask them to imagine going into their garden and yelling at the lettuce to grow! Usually this elicits a chuckle or two. It is silly to yell at ourselves for not suddenly emerging from the soil as a mature plant. Life is a process; we have only to enjoy the journey.

It Is Not as Simple as Simplifying

Books on the many ways of simplifying life are a hot item at bookstores. We researched many of these books in preparation for writing this book and found some excellent ideas for living a less complicated life. We also noted the exasperation of clients and friends who complain that redirecting their lives "is not as simple as simplifying." The movement to simplify life is a noble one, yet it misses the mark for many people. We began to wonder why and discovered that simplifying is part of a much bigger series of changes that must happen if we are to improve the quality of our lives.

Simplifying life requires an understanding of the values that direct life. Only when we discover what we value in life can we begin to determine what to maintain and what to leave behind. For instance, one gentleman threw off all his worldly possessions—in a massive garage sale—and left for three months to work and write in the Antarctic. His action was quick, impulsive, and accomplished with little forethought. Later, he admitted that his brash move cost him much more than he gained. Sudden changes may work for a precious few, but most of us benefit from change that rests in an understanding of our values and careful preparation for transformational actions.

Lasting Change Happens One Degree at a Time

Sometimes change is thrust on us in ways that propel us forward; however, most change, especially lasting change, happens in small increments. We often find, like the hapless frog, that negative change has slowly crept up on us. In the same way, changes that remove us from the boiling water happen, by and large, one degree at a time. The authors of the book *Changing for Good* (James O. Prochaska, Ph.D., John C. Norcross, Ph.D., and Carlos C. Diclemente, Ph.D.) cite a necessary step in the change process that many people overlook: preparation. Many of us forget to prepare for change and simply leap in a new direction, without considering the consequences that may result.

Lasting change usually rests on careful preparation. This calls for a more thoughtful way of living than our usual knee-jerk, reactive way. If we want to change in ways that improve our quality of life, we must understand how the heat became so intense, where we would rather be in our life, and how to prepare for the changes it will take to arrive at this new destination. This kind of change, which is satisfying and durable, usually happens slowly, one degree at a time.

Every Change Affects a Larger System

Every change you make to improve the quality of your life will have an effect on the larger systems around you. For instance, if you decide to improve your assertive communication, you will most certainly improve your relationships, your level of achievement, and your self-esteem. If you decide to improve your fitness, you will probably find yourself eating better foods, using your increased energy to accomplish more in other areas of your life, and feeling better about yourself all around. Every action you take will have a measurable consequence. Why not choose actions that are life affirming!

There is a saying in Western religion, "You reap what you sow." This is a life principle as well. Every action you take, great or small, will create a ripple effect of reactions in your life. This means that your personal growth will affect the world around you. When you become more congruent within, you have greater power and influence without. People who improve the quality of their own lives by improving the actions they take often have much to give and much more to gain!

The areas we address in this book operate in a system, each affecting the others. This is why we promote balance in each area. If you are out of synch in one area, it will affect the other areas. The following diagram illustrates how these areas work as a system.

The Quality-of-Life System

Life Management
Time
Information
Money
Burnout
Relationships
Community
Boundaries
Assertiveness
Partnership
Family
Positive Thinking
ABC reaction
Thinking error
Rehumanizing
Mind fitness
Good Health
Stress and illness
Nutrition
Fitness
Body image

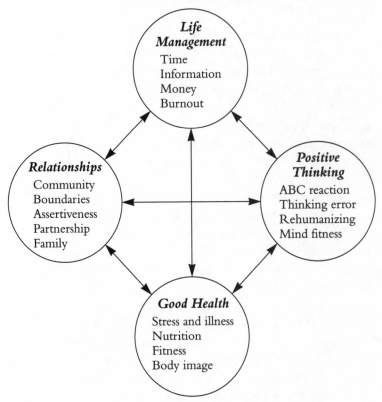

Love Is More than the Golden Rule

Most of us are familiar with the Golden Rule: "Do unto others as you would have them do unto you." We believe love is more than simply treating others the way you want to be treated. Love is giving more than equal treatment, especially in a society where some people do not benefit from the economic growth of the nation. In this case, love requires that those who have more, give more. It requires that citizens who have benefited from wealth, education, and special privileges associated with their gender, race, or religion give more of themselves to others.

There is an old parable about a spiritual master teaching a

starving man how to fish instead of producing enough food for him to eat at the moment. He explained to his disciples that if he simply fed the hungry man, the man would eat only for a day, but if he taught him to fish, he would eat for a lifetime. This is true generosity: helping those less fortunate learn to help themselves. This requires more than throwing money at a problem to ease a guilty conscience.

We believe that one reason the increase in Americans' personal wealth did not translate into an increase in charitable donations is related to the overwhelming number of requests for money on television, at work, and through telemarketing. It is frustrating to be assaulted by a dozen calls at night from various organizations asking for money. So what do you do? First of all, do not give up on giving. If the onslaught of nameless, faceless people calling you for money angers you, let the anger fuel a search for a name and face to put on your generosity. Find a way to roll up your sleeves and enter the problem with your heart as well as your wallet.

Practice Curiosity Instead of Judgment

How many times have you heard the old saying that curiosity killed the cat? It was a saying that kept many children from prying into things that adults believed were none of their business. It became a way of deadening a wonderful human trait: curiosity. Why did we not also hear that satisfaction of curiosity brought the cat back to the next of his nine lives? Instead of having our natural curiosity fostered, we learned to obey, to judge, and to measure things from a distance.

When we judge people or situations, we distance ourselves from opportunities to learn new ideas, to unravel great and small mysteries. Nowhere is this truer than in how we see ourselves. We have heard many clients and friends say, "No one is harder on me than me." This is why we encourage clients to be curious about the nuances that make up their individual person. When they say things like "I should . . . ," "I screwed up . . . ," or "I'm a failure," they are practicing judgment.

We encourage clients to keep a curiosity journal. When they make a mistake, they record the fascinating facts and insights that led up to the error. Instead of judging their behaviors, they foster a curiosity about what led them to their decisions. They find that whereas judgment was a dead-end street, curiosity leads them to wonderful new possibilities.

Life Happens—Only You Can Choose How You See It

Later in the book, we recommend that everyone take time each morning to reflect, pray, meditate, stare, or watch the sunrise. We believe that every morning we have a choice point for the day. We can take a few moments and truly set our course for the next ten to twelve hours, or we can race off and hope that things turn out okay. The latter path is one that most people choose. These people open their eyes and throw the day into automatic, letting habits and reactions determine the outcome.

We assume, because you are still reading this book, that you want a more conscious lifestyle, one that has you, not the day's events, at the helm. What if you decide to awaken tomorrow and set your own course for the day's journey? What if you were simply to say, "Today, I choose to live a life in which what I think aligns with what I say, aligns with what I feel, aligns with how I behave"? This is choosing heaven over hell, and the choice is yours and yours alone, every morning for the rest of your life. May it be a long one!

Part 1

TURNING DOWN THE HEAT ON TIME, INFORMATION, MONEY, AND BURNOUT

If we were not so single-minded

about keeping our lives moving,

and for once could do nothing,

perhaps a huge silence

might interrupt this sadness

of never understanding ourselves

and of threatening ourselves with death.

Perhaps the earth can teach us

as when everything seems dead

and later proves to be alive.

Pablo Neruda

This section is about turning down the heat in basic life areas such as time, information, money management, and burnout. For many of us, these problem areas may appear mundane, yet attending to the mundane is often the only way of making room for the truly profound moments of our lives. If we are caught up in worry about time, overload, stress, and money, where is the time for pleasure, peace of mind, and love for one another? ⚜ Chapter 2 focuses on the needs of the heart and the mind by helping you establish your priorities and values. Chapter 3 illustrates information overload, the basic truths of time, and principles of time management. Chapter 4 leads you through the myth that affluence brings happiness, explains how we are becoming a nation of debtors, and tells how to get a handle on your own finances. In Chapter 5, we discuss the timely subject of burnout: how to recognize the signs and how to mend from this modern malady. In the final chapter of the section, we discuss the many benefits of generosity, how to become a generous person, and how to teach your children the importance of giving.

Chapter 2

Balancing the Needs
of the Heart and Mind

_____

HUNG'S STORY: *Build a Life, Then Invite Someone In*

Hung is a rising star at his bank in downtown Denver. He is
an articulate, intelligent, first-generation Asian American.
Hung sought therapy because his girlfriend of three years left
him for a mutual friend. He was taken by surprise and mystified by her sudden departure. Hung came to the session with
his pager, cell phone, and laptop in tow. He handled them
with a kind of fluidity that suggested they had become ap-
pendages. Several times during the session his pager vibrated
and he apologized for interrupting with "just one more call."
By the end of the half-hour session, Hung had spent half of
his time responding to his modern "conveniences."

Hung agreed not to answer his pager at the next session. It
was apparent that this was not an easy commitment for him.
At the next session, he tensed at every pager vibration and his
breathing became shallow. Once he turned off the pager, he
relaxed. As he relaxed, his youth began to show. He shrugged
his shoulders like a young boy when asked why he believed
his girlfriend had left. He softened as he talked about her, a
painter who was also a first-generation Asian American. He
obviously loved her deeply. Hung was asked to complete an
inventory exercise at home that would describe the pieces of

his life like slices of a pie—the more time spent in each area, the bigger the slice.

At his next session, Hung came in and shared his inventory. His pie consisted of one huge slice and several tiny ones. The biggest slice was his career at the bank; the smaller ones consisted of his music (he was a classically trained pianist), his social time, and his family time. When asked where his girlfriend had fit in, he fumbled with the question. Hung looked at the pie and slumped in his chair. "It would appear there is no room for her in my life," he said quietly. The room was silent for several minutes as Hung gazed at his life. "What a fool," he muttered.

There is a saying, "Humility is teachability and open-mindedness to the truth." We must be willing to examine old patterns in order to change and grow. Hung was willing to acknowledge that his priorities were not meeting his needs. He was feeling the painful awareness that initiates life changes for so many clients. He was also willing to take the time and make the effort to build a life and then invite someone else into it. Hung did not win back his girlfriend. Therapy seldom offers a Hollywood ending. But Hung did find another wonderful woman about a year later. He invited her into a life with room for a relationship. Today, they both struggle at times, successfully balancing career and family while balancing the needs of the mind and the heart.

WHAT ARE YOUR PRIORITIES?

The following exercise helped Hung reevaluate his life. He listed the most important things in his life and how many hours per week he spent on each. In this way, he was able to see where his priorities were not being supported by his lifestyle. Take a moment to list your top priorities and write down how many hours per week you spend attending to each of these.

Top Priorities	*Hours Spent Per Week*
_____	_____
_____	_____
_____	_____
_____	_____
_____	_____
_____	_____
_____	_____
_____	_____
_____	_____

Now, Hung could come up with ways to balance his life in a way that supported the things that mattered most to him. The second exercise helped Hung create a pie chart to illustrate the time he wanted to spend on various activities. Now that he knew what was most important to him, it became easier to create a balanced chart. The following examples of pie charts are from clients who worked diligently to rearrange their lives in a way that reflected their top priorities.

Hung's Pie Chart

17

James's Pie Chart

Linda's Pie Chart

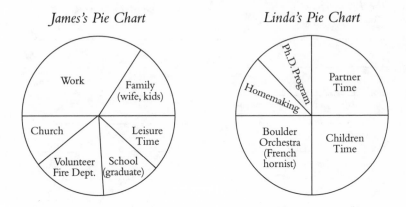

CREATE YOUR PIE CHART

In the circle on the left, divide your life into sections, like pieces of a pie, according to what percentage of time you spend on various activities. Include work, family time, partnership time, leisure, relaxation, exercise, watching television, and so on. Next, create a pie chart in the circle on the right that divides your time in the way you would like it to be. Be sure to include most of your list of top priorities. This chart represents the direction in which you want to go with your life.

Current Pie Chart

What You Really Want!

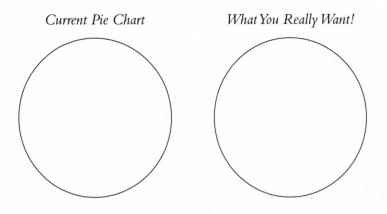

JOAN AND DAVID'S STORY: *Dropping In Before You Drop Out*

Joan and David were burned out. Whatever American dream they had thought they would reach by age forty still eluded them. One day they decided to drop out, pack up, and move to a small mountain town in Colorado. They exchanged a $260,000 income as advertising executives, a swank home on Manhattan's East Side, and a high-society lifestyle for a $40,000 income and a modest home in a small-town community. As springtime in the Rockies brought wildflowers, blue skies, and clean mountain air, Joan and David's spirits soared. One year later, their marriage had collapsed under mountain snows, terminal boredom, and an isolated community. Joan left David, landed a job at an advertising agency in Denver, and ended up in one of our seminars.

This couple's well-intentioned solution to the stresses of their lives was to drop out. In fact, they exchanged one problem for another. As the saying goes, wherever you go, there *you* are. There is a trend toward dropping out, slowing down, and trying to simplify one's life. Yet for many people the solution is not as simple as merely simplifying. We counsel clients who are considering extreme changes along the lines of Joan and David's to drop in before they drop out. Here's what we mean.

At our seminar, Joan discovered she valued the excitement and intensity of New York. The social isolation of the small town made her feel unexpectedly lonely. She dropped back into city life, this time in downtown Denver, and found what she really wanted. She left New York looking for simplicity and went too far. She didn't want the country life; she just wanted life in a city smaller than New York. She had taken the pendulum too far in the other direction. It may be helpful to stop and think about what you really value before you make drastic changes. This requires dropping in, not dropping out.

How do you create meaning in the here and now? You do this by identifying your values, determining how well your life expresses those values, and changing the areas that are not aligned with them. Sounds simple? Well, it's not. Dropping out is simple; it's a simplistic solution for a complicated problem. In Joan's case, it cost her her marriage. Who knows what it cost David.

VALUES CLARIFICATION

You have already created a list of top priorities. How do you know if these priorities are ones you truly value? You know this if the priority fulfills at least one of your values. What is a value? A value is something that matters to you, like good health. Many of us confuse values with activities or things that support the value. For instance, let's say you value good health, but you say you value fitness. Good health is the value; maintaining your fitness is one way you support this value.

Many people list money as a value. Money is actually a way of supporting something more fundamental. For instance, you may want money because it will pay your bills and give you peace of mind. Peace of mind is the actual value; money supports this value. Below we have listed some general values for you to consider when compiling your personal list.

Success	*Love*	*Power*	*Adventure*
Serenity	*Service*	*Health*	*Community*
Intimacy	*Harmony*	*Peace*	*Spirituality*

On the lines below, list your values. Include any of the values listed above that fit your life and any others you can think of.

_____

_____

_____

_____

_____

_____

Next, circle your top four values on the list and write them in order of importance under the heading, "My Top Four" below. In the space provided, list any items or activities you have in your life now that support each of these values. For example, if you value serenity and you meditate or pray, this would be a way your life supports that value. This exercise will allow you to evaluate how well your current lifestyle supports your values.

My Top Four   *Items or Activities That Support This Value*

1 _____   _____

2 _____   _____

3 _____   _____

4 _____   _____

Remember, as you continue to revise this list over the course of your life, values are at the root of everything you think, feel, and do in life. Our goal is to help you discover the link between your values and how they align with what you say, which aligns with what you feel, which aligns with how you behave. To achieve this alignment is to have integrity, which is a cornerstone to living a quality life!

Chapter 3

Information Overload

TAMAR'S STORY: *Tamar Has a Secret*

Tamar entered therapy complaining of anxiety attacks and insomnia. She is a forty-year-old Israeli American who works as a computer analyst in a major U.S. software company and lives with her husband and two children in a wealthy suburb of Denver. In the first session, she reports fearing that her brain is about to spontaneously combust. She has a sense of humor. That's a good sign. Tamar has a highly organized life, with every ten minutes carefully planned in her voluminous appointment book. Tamar spends the entire session explaining in great detail the entire group of daily tasks and appointments that make up a typical day in her life. Her sense of control and timing are astounding—disturbingly so.

In all the details, information, and busyness of a typical day, Tamar is burying a truth about her life. The first task of therapy is to help her slow down and take a belly breath. On her fifth belly breath, tears begin to stream from her dark eyes. She becomes frightened and starts to hold her breath, but the tears continue—a lifetime of tears.

Tamar has a secret. Before she can build the motivation to slow her life down, she must face the fear of what will surface in the still moments. She must face her secret. Slowly the truth emerges and she whispers, "I don't think I love my husband anymore." The statement hangs in the silence as her tears turn into gut-wrenching sobs.

Her anxiety attacks are no longer a mystery. Her attention to detail and her information overload are a carefully crafted defense against a painful truth about her marriage of fifteen years. When she drops her hands, it appears as if ten years have disappeared from her delicate features. She begins to talk more about the pain, the disappointment, and the guilt.

How could she leave her faithful partner? Break up her happy family? Disrupt the lives of her kids? It will take time, but Tamar will come to understand that her children are not really happy with a mom in perpetual motion and with a cool distance growing between her and their father. Her husband will recover. He deserves, as does Tamar, to be married to someone who loves him.

Tamar's story is becoming all too common in therapy sessions. A culturally supported busyness has taken over the lives of many clients. Sometimes it is a life that slowly, imperceptibly speeds up. Sometimes it is a semiconscious decision not to face a truth by staying busy. Remember the boiling frog in the introduction? His stresses increased one degree at a time. In Tamar's case, the degrees are represented by each little task she adds to her life until her stress level reaches a boiling point and spills over.

Tamar is not alone with her burden of too much input. Most of us live in an age of information overload: News stories are repeated continuously on radio, television, the Internet, and newspapers; more books are published every year than we will ever have time to know about, let alone read. Technology comes with increasingly complex and time-consuming instructions, while many of us still struggle with the seemingly simple task of setting our VCR timers!

Through our work with clients we have come to realize how a person's stress builds with each new technological breakthrough and each breaking news story; the details are be-coming increasingly difficult to keep up with. In this chapter, we pass along the most effective ways we have found to deal with the speed and intensity of American life.

Over the years many of us have been seduced out of align-ment by lifestyles propelled by material gain and an increasing need for speed. Sadly, some of us have found ourselves think-ing one thing, telling each other something else, and behaving in ways that match neither. So where are we going in such a hurry, so laden with treasures? A lot of us no longer know. The journey has become a race for someplace, anyplace, as long as it is not this place, this time. We lose the only moment that matters, the one happening here and now.

There is a lack of self-responsibility when we let our lives begin to live us. Tamar is certainly not alone in her life. Infor-mation overload and time mismanagement dominate Ameri-can life. Personal integrity entails slowing down and facing the kind of truth that emerges in moments of calm and quiet.

BASIC TRUTHS OF TIME

We need not only to understand how we mismanage time; we need to change our entire relationship with time. This happens when we learn the basic truths of time. It's not only how we use time that matters; it's how we view time. By knowing more about time, we can learn to master how we relate to it in our daily lives. Following are some basic truths about this thing we call time.

Make Time for Nothing

There is a strange paradox concerning time management. The more time you take to do nothing, the more time you will have for all things. People often fall into two camps: those who have little time and are constantly rushing everywhere, and those who have too much empty time and feel stuck and iso-lated. If we take a few minutes a day, preferably in the morning, to sit quietly, we begin to move through the rest of our day with greater ease and serenity.

Tamar did not uncover the truth about her life until she slowed down and checked inside. She made a commitment to set her alarm fifteen minutes earlier than usual. She used these extra minutes to sit in a chair and stare out her living-room window at the rising sun. When her children awakened, she was much calmer and more relaxed and ready to begin her day.

You can do the same. Try this today: Simply sit and listen to the quiet. It doesn't matter what you call this ritual: prayer, meditation, quiet time, staring, or stillness. The important thing is to give yourself some time each morning. Try to take this time when you will be undisturbed by your family, the phone, or morning news. The results will amaze you!

The Seasonal Nature of Time

One way to step out of the human calendar is to create a seasonal lifestyle. Consider incorporating seasonal behaviors and rituals into your yearly cycle. Performing seasonal rituals can create a natural rhythm and help you feel connected to something larger than the artificial concept of time. Consider what you notice the natural world doing seasonally. For example, in the fall the trees shed their leaves, squirrels gather nuts, and days grow shorter.

In the space provided on page 27, create a list of human behaviors that might conform to these seasons. For example, harvesting a garden in the fall, slowing down in the winter, cleaning your home in the spring, having a picnic in the summer. Incorporate these rituals into your life and watch how you begin to view time more naturally and serenely.

Fall

_____

_____

_____

Winter

_____

_____

_____

Spring

_____

_____

_____

Summer

_____

_____

_____

Slowing Down Equals More Time

Tamar could not grasp that slowing down creates time when she first came to therapy. Once she found what she truly wanted in life, it began to make more sense. You too may wonder how this could be true. After all, if you slow down, you'll be late, you won't have time to do something else later, or you won't have time to rest. Hurry, hurry, hurry! STOP!!

Hurrying and worrying about time create stress. Stress in

your body creates illness. Do it long enough and you might die! If you die, you really lose time! This is the simple truth about slowing down. If you slow down, you will reduce stress. If you reduce stress, you will live longer. If you live longer, you will certainly have more time. So, slowing down equals more time.

MIKE'S STORY: *Trapped in the News*

Mike is a news junkie. He reads the paper over breakfast, listens to public radio on his way to and from work, and watches CNN throughout the evening. In his spare time, he surfs the Internet. Mike is particularly interested in news stories about the environment. In chat rooms on the Internet, he and other surfers lament the demise of the planet. He subscribes to numerous major environmental newsletters, magazines, and action networks. In his session, he describes a litany of sins humans are committing against the earth and how he hates the hypocrisy of our times. Under his vehement speeches, Mike is sinking deeper into a lifelong depression. He is a man full of the problems and burdens of his planet. He is not alone. The news of what we are doing to our environment comes at such a fast and furious rate in our media it is paralyzing many people's ability to respond. As a result of this kind of information overload, Mike and many others sink into a "learned helplessness" that precludes action and invites depression.

One problem with information overload is that it often renders us powerless in the face of frightening global problems. Mike manifests this powerlessness in his increasing depression and anger at faceless corporations, politicians, and religious leaders. His world of dissatisfaction is enormous compared to the everyday scope of his life as a computer programmer. He is a man trapped in the news.

Mike's first assignment was to unplug. For one week, every other day, Mike was to avoid any news of the world. He kept a journal of his moods for that week. When he returned to his next session, Mike was in knots. It was a good sign. He found that on his unplugged days, he was incredibly anxious. On his Net-surfing, news-watching days, he was in an energized rage, a state sometimes called an *agitated depression*.

The problems Mike experienced were a kind of information overload. Because of the time spent on the Internet, he heard too much, he saw too much, he took in *too much*. We have talked about how information overload is on the rise in this society. It can be especially dangerous for people who spend their workday at the computer and then come home to surf the net. All computers and no play make for a very unbalanced life.

Mike was also a news junky. News junkies hang on every detail of the latest plane crash, presidential misfire, or world crisis. Wow! How many times do you suppose they hear the same stories? How many times does their blood pressure rise at a tragic story that plays six times a day? Most important, how much time do they spend listening to the same news instead of enjoying themselves?

Mike kept a log documenting time spent following the news as well as a wish list of secret hopes and dreams. He was amazed at the hours each day spent focusing on the news of the world. Once Mike weaned himself off the news, he found hope in the hours available to devote to his wish list.

The next step was to encourage Mike to use some of his un-plugged days looking for ways to become actively involved in his concerns about the environment. He found many ways to plug into the local environmental movement. To his surprise, he found there are ways to become part of the solution as op-posed to sitting at home, isolated, and obsessing about the problem.

COMPENSATORY LEISURE

Balance happens when people engage in "compensatory leisure" after work. In short, they use leisure time to compensate for the tasks done at the office. For instance, if you work with computers, use your leisure time to garden, exercise, play with your children, make love, cook dinner for your friends, or go to a movie. Here is a challenge. Do not go home and log onto the Net! We believe that life is about balancing the needs of your mind and your heart in order to have happiness and good health.

Take a moment to list your tasks at work, either at the office or at home, in the left-hand column of the following chart. These might include typing, making phone calls, computer work, listening to others, writing, working inside all day, changing diapers, chauffeuring kids, cleaning house, cooking, and so on. Directly across from these activities, match leisure activities that might compensate for your work activities.

For instance, if you spend the day with kids, you may want to be alone or to go out with adults in the evening. If you are inside all day, you may want to walk in the evenings. Let your imagination go, and find what would truly compensate for and balance out your work activities.

Work Activities	*Leisure Activities to Compensate*
_____	_____
_____	_____
_____	_____
_____	_____
_____	_____
_____	_____
_____	_____

_____   _____

_____   _____

_____   _____

_____   _____

_____   _____

_____   _____

It is not simply our leisure time that needs attention. There are many things in our lives that can lead to poor time management. The kind of information overload that Mike experienced is just one of them. Lack of balance is a common thread. Mike was overly focused on the news of the world, but others of us spend an inordinate amount of time on our cars, the lawn, our jobs. If we want balance in our lives, we must take charge of balancing our time in ways that make us multidimensional people.

MORE BASIC TRUTHS ABOUT TIME

Poor time management is a common complaint. Here are a few more basic truths about time for you to incorporate into your routine. These changes alone will greatly improve your relationship with time.

Develop Time Managers

Organize your home. Many of us waste a lot of time searching for things we've misplaced. It doesn't have to be that way. The old adage "a place for everything and everything in its place" reminds us to save time spent needlessly hunting for misplaced articles. Here are some essentials for home organization:

1. Use a filing system for bills, documents, and paper.
2. Designate a location for daily mail.
3. Place bills in order in a mail file.

4. Use a corkboard or sticky notes to post reminders and to-do lists.

5. When possible, use rooms for the purpose the name indicates. For example, don't have your office in your bedroom or kitchen.

6. Get in the habit of spring-cleaning.

Purchase an Appointment Book

Find one that fits you best. One client of ours picked out a cartoon calendar book to remind herself to lighten up about time and all the appointments in her life. Use your book to schedule things you *have* to do. Also, schedule in the things you *want* to do. If your book shows your obligations and also your adventures, you'll use it! Use it to schedule time with yourself: time to meditate, time for adventure, time for personal development, time to hang out with friends, and time for nothing.

Help Someone Every Day

It could be as simple as opening a door for someone carrying too many packages. Other options include dropping by to visit a sick friend, sending a flower to a loved one, or volunteering at a local charity. It could be a phone call to someone who'd love to hear from you. One simple act of kindness each day will be returned when you need it most.

For People in a Hurry, Schedule in More Time

If you are someone who rushes everywhere you go, this tip is for you. When you write an appointment or activity in your appointment book, add a few minutes to the beginning and end of each entry. Give yourself one hour to make a forty-five-minute drive. If you give yourself fifteen minutes to meditate, try adding another five to ten minutes.

For People Who Procrastinate, Just Do It

Take one thing you have been putting off, large or small, and do it. Now! Today! Curing procrastination takes a commitment to break the habit. It doesn't have to be huge. You can wake up tomorrow and put a stamp on the letter that has been sitting by the phone for two weeks. You will be surprised at the relief and self-confidence that will build with every action you take. One day you will wake up and find you are no longer a person who puts things off, but a person who feels the satisfaction of getting things done.

THE TWELVE PRINCIPLES OF TIME MANAGEMENT

1. *The 80/20 rule.* Simply stated, this rule says that only 20 percent of the things we do produces 80 percent of the rewards. This means that focusing on high-priority items will be the best plan for reaching your goals.

2. *Saying no.* Learn to say no. Unless it is absolutely essential to do something, stay away from low-priority or unimportant tasks. Be prepared to say that you do not have the time. Practice your assertive communication skills.

3. *Delegate when possible.* Many low-priority tasks can be done by others: an assistant, partner, someone you hire, your children, and so forth.

4. *Use rewards.* Reinforce any successes you have as you complete your task. This could be a gift to yourself, dinner on the town, flowers for your desk or table, a massage, a cooking lesson, a subscription to a favorite magazine, a new compact disc or cassette, a nice long bath, or sleeping an extra hour.

5. *Use a to-do list.* Maintain a daily to-do list monitoring your activities toward your stated goals. Divide larger goals into subgoals and put these on your list. Keep your entries in order of importance.

6. *Use a "not to do" list.* Make lists of activities you know are time-wasters. For example, do not get distracted with phone calls when focusing on an important task.

7. *Use reminders.* Our memories are often faulty, and using written reminders about particular tasks keeps us from let-

ting important things slide. Reminders can be valuable aids.

8. *The "bits and pieces" approach.* Begin an important project and work on it as long as possible. Do part of it. Make a start. Whittle away larger projects to smaller ones. Bits of work add up over the long haul.

9. *Ride the momentum.* Once you start a task, you may find you can go with the momentum generated and either do more than you thought you could or begin an additional task. For example, you might start cleaning your home and find that you are motivated to sort and give away old clothing.

10. *The ten-minute plan.* Using this method, you can build initial momentum. Agree to start a task, but contract to spend only ten minutes on it. At the end of that time, ask yourself whether you want to spend another ten minutes on it. Most people find once they have begun a task, they can continue longer than they originally estimated.

11. *Do it when you think of it.* Often, the best time to do something is when you think of it, rather than postponing it for later. Paying a bill now means you will not have to go through the hassle of finding it a second time.

12. *Schedule.* Once you have determined the appropriate activities for accomplishing a job, schedule time to carry them out. Try to schedule activities at times when you are most effective and most likely to achieve your goals.

Chapter 4

The Age of Affluence
or the Age of Debt?

PLANO'S STORY: *The Age of Affluenza*

Several years ago reports hit the national press of tragedies rocking Plano, a small upscale community in Texas. In this well-to-do suburb over a dozen high-school students had died of heroin overdoses. These students were not outcasts, nor were they delinquents. One was a cheerleader, one a star football player, another a straight-A student . . . and the list goes on. It shocked the town. Explanations were necessary. One mother's reasoning made sense to us. She was on the *Oprah Winfrey Show* one afternoon telling of her attempts to save her son. She had tried to help her son beat his addiction. Finally, she had him arrested for drug possession so he could receive the help he needed. Oprah asked the parents who were guests why they thought this tragedy had happened. This mother replied eloquently that she believed parents were teaching kids how to get and how to accumulate, and forgetting to teach them how to give and reach out to others. She was waking up and getting herself and her family out of the hot water.

This mother hits on a central theme of our book: that affluence can be destructive. Some writers have referred to these heady times as the age of affluenza, as if too much affluence is like a nasty case of the flu. How did we get here? One degree at a time.

We certainly do not promote taking a vow of poverty as a means to happiness, though some people have done that successfully. We want simply to note how seductive money and possessions can be. Contrary to the advertising messages we are bombarded with, affluence does not equal happiness. One reason money does not bring happiness is that it often has nothing to do with what we value. Living a life based on what we value is the key to happiness. The client in the next story personifies the type of American who becomes seduced by affluence and then drowns in the demands for more and more.

ALEX'S STORY: *The Banker in Foreclosure*

It is no surprise to see another foreclosure sign going up on a street in Boulder. Foreclosure and bankruptcy are becoming all too familiar in our communities throughout the country. What is surprising is that the owner of this house, Alex, is a forty-seven-year-old investment banker with a national lending institution. He makes a six-figure income, owns a luxurious home, and has three kids in college; his wife makes a good income as a mediation expert. Here's how it happened. Alex bought a home slightly over his earning potential. When he was still giddy from his move into the high life, banks started sending him credit cards with limits of $10,000 to $100,000 at initial interest rates as low as 4.9 percent. He began to charge little amounts here and there and pretty soon had a debt of $50,000 on top of his mortgage of $750,000. Things were tight at first, but when the card interest rates skyrocketed to 18 percent after six months, the debt started piling up. Next, he started receiving invitations to refinance his home. He did that, taking out all of the existing equity. The spending continued. When two of his children came home to report they had also accumulated $25,000 in credit card debt, Alex knew he was in trouble. It was too late to save the house, the cars, and the kids' college funds. In twelve short months, he lost his family's lifetime savings.

Does this story sound familiar? Whether we're earning $17,000 a year or $70,000 a year, we can find ourselves in Alex's shoes. Studies show the average credit card debt for each American has risen to $8,000. That is an astounding figure. We have become a nation of debtors. When the debt becomes too large, many turn to the easy solution of bankruptcy. Where is our sense of fiscal responsibility? When did we come to believe in some ultimate rescuer to bail us out of our troubles? Once again we are being seduced. The cool water of easy credit slowly heats up until it is too late to jump. This chapter is about waking up to financial responsibility and taking charge of our own money.

STAYING OUT OF DEBT: STEPS TO FINANCIAL BALANCE

There's a little paperback called *The Richest Man in Babylon* (by George S. Clason) that's a classic in money management. In this book, the author cites three valuable keys to financial success:

1. Save 10 percent of every dollar you earn—before taxes.
2. Place 10 percent on your debts (i.e., car and house payments).
3. Donate 10 percent to charity.

These three principles guide the financial success of some of the richest people in the world.

Here are some other guidelines for money management:

1. Pay off your credit cards each and every month; do not carry a balance on any card.

2. Create a monthly and yearly budget for your household and stick to it. It is crucial to learn to live within your means.

3. Plan for your retirement. If you don't have an individual retirement account, open one as soon as possible.

4. Carry health insurance; a medical condition could easily wipe out your savings.

5. Create savings accounts for future purchases and contribute to them monthly. Include these contributions in your monthly budget.

6. If you keep running up credit card debt, here is a story for you. A client shared this creative way she manages to keep her hands off the credit cards except for emergencies. She places her cards in baggies full of water and sticks them in the freezer. This makes impulsive shopping more difficult for her.

7. Establish a date and time, twice each month, to pay bills. Do this as a couple, if you are in a relationship.

8. When a bill comes in the mail, try either of these options:
   A. Using a rubber stamp, write the due date on each bill. Then place the bill in an open file on your desk.
   B. Create a "tickler" file using an accordion file case. Mark the separate dividers with the numbers one through thirty-one. Place bills in the divider that corresponds to the date when the bill is due, allowing for mailing time. (Tickler files are great for remembering birthdays too. Just buy a card when you think of it, and keep it in the file on the person's birth date.)

9. Become "financially literate." Instead of working for money, learn to make your money work for you. We recommend the following books to get you started on financial literacy:

   Rich Dad, Poor Dad by Robert T. Kiyosaki
   The E-Myth by Michael Gerber
   The Discipline of Market Leaders by Michael Treacy and Frederik D. Wiersema

According to authors like Kiyosaki, the financial advice of our parents is no longer feasible in our fast-changing world. Learning basic elements such as the difference between an asset and a liability are key concepts to financial mastery in the twenty-first century. Remember, financial mastery equals lower stress, which equals higher quality of life!

If you find yourself in a difficult financial situation, you may feel like the weight of the world is on your shoulders. It is easy to ignore the problem until it is so big it takes you under. Wake up, but don't despair. Read on!

JASON AND MEGAN'S STORY: *Where Has All the Money Gone?*

Jason and Megan came into couples counseling after a bitter quarrel that left them both thinking about divorce. In the interview they discussed many typical issues of couples in conflict: poor communication skills, inability to maintain separate identities, and money problems. They ranked their issues as to how much stress each one caused to the relationship. Money topped the list. Jason and Megan were slowly going into debt, and instead of dealing with the problem they spent their time blaming one another. Neither one had any idea where all their hard-earned money had gone.

It is easy for couples to slip into inaction around money issues, especially if they spend energy blaming each other for the problem. Blame often precludes self-responsibility. In addition, many couples spend money as a couple, not as two independent, fiscally responsible adults. The two people dissolve into a merged "we." Jason and Megan would often speak of their money issues in terms of a boundaryless "we": "We can't seem to save money." "We are $12,000 in debt." "We keep spending money we don't have." It is hard to address this person named "we," because it does not exist. The task of the therapist became twofold: to help them separate their individual responsibility and to assign them separate tasks to address the financial crisis.

Money issues like Jason and Megan's are common complaints of our clients. Often, these individuals and couples do not have a clue where the money they work so hard to earn goes at the end of every pay period. It is a mystery they must solve before they can learn to live within their means.

When a couple presents the kinds of issues Megan and Jason do, the first step is to eliminate the pronoun *we*. Each time they started a statement with *we,* they were asked to use the pronoun *I* instead. They were also instructed to present only how they personally managed money, not how they saw the other doing it. Soon, Jason and Megan were able to identify their individual weaknesses around money and work to change them.

The first assignment they were given was to divide the task of accounting for the money they both spent in the last three months. Jason agreed to break down the checkbook expenditures by category. Megan agreed to do the same with credit card charges. They were given a week to accomplish this and come back with a three-month expenditure list.

Jason and Megan came to their next session displaying a mixture of anxiety and wonder. They were astonished at where the money had gone in the last three months. They were able to see the essential expenses of their lifestyle and the frivolous ones. For once, they were not pointing fingers at each other nor calling up the mysterious "we." The responsibility was sitting on the table in front of them. Now, they could truly begin to master their finances.

Their next assignment was to clarify their personal values and prioritize their expenditures. They followed the values clarification exercise explained in Chapter 2. After this, they were each instructed to take a copy of the expenditure list and go through the following steps. The first step was to circle the expenditures on their list that were necessary or fixed monthly items. These included payments for the house, car, utilities, food, medical needs, and so on. These were to be placed on a separate page as Level 1 expenses. Then they were asked to use their top five values to arrange the rest of the expenditures in three descending levels of priority.

When they came back to therapy, Jason and Megan were asked to tell one another what expenditures were in each of their levels of priority. There were many surprises for both when they heard the differences in what they valued being spoken aloud. And they were equally surprised at the many common values and priorities they had as a couple. Next, it was a matter of deciding if they could actually pay for their list of wants and needs.

Jason and Megan began by subtracting the costs of taxes, retirement contributions, savings, debt, and charity from their monthly incomes. Then they subtracted their fixed expenses (Level 1). Finally, they subtracted Level 2, Level 3, and Level 4 expenses. They came up with a deficit of $1,000 each month. The mystery of their $12,000 debt accumulated over the last year was solved. Now came the hard part. Jason and Megan needed to agree to deduct $500 each from their monthly budget. It created some anger, tears, and frustration, but soon they were able to reach a compromise. They each found things they could live without. And they found that what they did not want to live without was each other.

NOW IT'S YOUR TURN

Accomplishing the task of staying within your budget can be empowering. Here are five simple steps to get you started. If you are a couple, please divide the responsibilities like Jason and Megan did.

Step 1

Even if you think you know where all your money is going, do this step first. You may be surprised at what you find.

• Go through all your receipts and/or canceled checks from

the last three months and categorize the expenses.
- If you don't know what categories to use, check out the ones in computer budgeting programs and other budget or tax-reporting books. The categories include costs for housing, utilities, food, entertainment, education, phone, auto, and so on.

Step 2

- Circle the items on your expenditure list that are fixed, meaning they occur and must be paid every month. This includes items such as house and auto loans. These are Level 1 expenses.
- Take a moment to relist your values, referring to your values clarification exercise, in the space provided at the top of the following expenditure priority list.
- Next write your Level 1 expenditures and their monthly costs in the appropriate columns. The first level will contain the fixed expenses.
- Then fill in the Level 2, 3, and 4 expenses and the monthly cost of each.

EXPENDITURE PRIORITY LIST

MY VALUES: _____ _____ _____ _____

Level 1 Expenditures　　　　　　*Monthly Cost of*
(Fixed Expenses)　　　　　　　　*Expenditure*

_____　　　　_____

_____　　　　_____

_____　　　　_____

_____　　　　_____

_____   _____

_____   _____

_____   _____

_____   _____

_____   _____

*Total Cost*_____

Level 2 Expenditures
(Variable yet need; e.g., gas)

Monthly Cost of
Expenditure

_____   _____

_____   _____

_____   _____

_____   _____

_____   _____

_____   _____

_____   _____

_____   _____

*Total Cost*_____

Level 3 Expenditures
(Variable wants; e.g., clothes)

Monthly Cost of
Expenditure

_____   _____

_____   _____

_____   _____

_____   _____

_____   _____

_____   _____

_____   _____

_____   _____

_____   _____

Total Cost_____

Level 4 Expenditures   *Monthly Cost of*
(Entertainment)   *Expenditure*

_____   _____

_____   _____

_____   _____

_____   _____

_____   _____

_____   _____

_____   _____

Total Cost_____

Step 3

Now it is time to take account of your income.

- Place your current monthly income on the line provided below. There are some deductions you will need to account for before you move to your level of expenses.
- First, subtract the cost of your estimated taxes and your retirement funds.
- Next, subtract 10 percent for savings, 10 percent for debts such as additional payment on car(s) or home, and 10 percent for charity (unless you choose to give of your time rather than money).
- If you have a credit card debt that is too large to pay off in one month, increase your debt percentage so you can recover from this debt within a year or two. Make a promise to yourself to STOP USING YOUR CREDIT CARDS!

Monthly income   _____

Minus taxes   —   _____

Adjusted income   _____

Minus retirement   —   _____

Adjusted income   _____

Minus 10 percent for savings   —   _____

Adjusted income   _____

Minus 10 percent for
debts such as car(s) or home   —   _____

Adjusted income   _____

Minus 10 percent for charity — _____

Adjusted income _____

- Now you have your actual monthly income for your budget.
- Next, subtract all Level 1 expenses from your monthly budget.
- Then, subtract your Level 2 expenses and so on until you have all monthly expenses accounted for.

Actual income left for expenses _____

Minus Level 1 expenses — _____

Adjusted income _____

Minus Level 2 expenses — _____

Adjusted income _____

Minus Level 3 expenses — _____

Adjusted income _____

Minus Level 4 expenses — _____

Final total + or — _____

Step 4

- If your monthly expenses are greater than your monthly income, it is time to begin a realistic budget.
- Make a note of how much you are spending over your income each month.
- Then start with your Level 4 expenses to find out if eliminating any or all of them will cover this cost overrun.

- Continue to Level 3 expenses and so on until you can balance your income and expenses.

Try to remember that the stress of debt far exceeds the sacrifices you need to make to live within your means. You might want to rotate the items you eliminate every month. For instance, one month you may decide to cut your entertainment expense in half, and the following month it could be your clothes allowance instead.

Once you have this discrepancy between income and expenses corrected, you have created a budget to live by. It takes discipline and maturity to stick to a budget, but the rewards of financial security far outweigh any initial sacrifices you may have to make. Financial stability greatly enhances one's quality of life.

Chapter 5

Stress and Burnout

LESLIE'S STORY: *Crispy Fried*

Leslie is a hard worker. She derives a great deal of her personal identity from being a driven manager who seldom makes mistakes. Her competence has earned her the praises of her bosses and increasing responsibilities during the downsizing of her company. However, the company does not pay her any more for the increased workload. When Leslie starts to feel exhausted and overworked, she reminds herself of an old saying of her mother's: "Don't get a lighter pack, get a stronger back." It's no surprise that Leslie takes on new responsibilities without complaining, staying late at night and working on the weekends. Last month, Leslie's performance review was below average. She was devastated and pledged to work even harder, but her performance kept spiraling downward. Leslie ended up becoming ill and depressed and was put on notice by her boss that she could not rely on her past success. The company could not afford to keep her much longer. It all happened one degree at a time.

Leslie described her mornings as a juggling act. She felt like the juggler she saw once on the Ed Sullivan Show who kept about a dozen plates twirling on the ends of individual sticks. This juggler barely had time to keep the last plate from falling when the first one needed his attention. Leslie felt that her life had become just like this exhausting balancing act.

Burnout occurs when your efforts begin to outweigh the rewards that you derive from these efforts. In Leslie's case, she was expected to work harder, with more responsibilities and longer hours, but there was no increase in the reward. This is a common complaint when downsizing occurs in a company. Often, middle managers like Leslie suffer the most from the restructuring of their company.

Leslie decided to take two weeks' leave from the company to regain her physical and emotional health. When she returned to work, she asserted her need for an assistant to absorb some of her extra workload. She found a way to join with her boss, by imagining the best about her and seeing that she also was overworked and underpaid. Leslie tallied her work hours at sixty per week and was provided with a part-time assistant to help with the overload. She reminded the boss that training someone new for her job would cost the company far more than the wages of a managerial assistant. She turned down the heat and was able to stay with her company.

The workplace is one area of life that can lead to burnout; raising children is another. Many new parents complain that they seem to have more and more to do and less and less time in which to do it. Certainly the rewards of child rearing are many; however, the stress of parenting can lead to burned-out Moms and Dads who find their patience tested on a daily basis. Many parents forget to take care of themselves; some have limited resources in terms of money, social support, and time. The heat begins to rise until parents find themselves snapping and yelling at their children and at each other.

SELF-REGULATION

You have read about the many ways that our society pressures us to do more, achieve more, and acquire more. Most of these attainments bring greater responsibilities and burdens—that is the part many of us forget to take into account. Maybe the house on the hill is your dream, but is it worth the way you burn out in order to make the payments? Maybe having five kids seems like a terrific idea, but do you have the resources to support all five of these little beings? The new job title may fill you with pride, but does it bring enough rewards to balance out all the new pressures? If you answer yes to these questions, great!

If you hesitate, go back and reexamine your values clarification exercise. Make sure the added pressures in your life support what is important to you. If not, you just might end up like Leslie. Often clients complain that life is unfair and this or that aspect of their life overwhelms them. Change occurs when they begin to accept responsibility for regulating their lives. After all, who is in charge of our appointment books? Who makes the decisions to burden our lives with greater numbers of activities and possessions? When we take responsibility for the decisions we have made, we release the energy to make new, more informed decisions to relieve the pressure and turn down the heat.

SIGNS OF BURNOUT

We help our clients discover their natural ability to self-regulate—to notice when they are out of balance and make the appropriate corrections. The first step is to recognize the signs that they are feeling burned out and out of balance. Many of the signs of burnout are confused with signs of illness, mental or physical.

For instance, major depression can be defined by symptoms such as confusion, uncontrollable crying, or exhaustion. These are also symptoms of burnout. How could this be? Sometimes depression is functional, meaning it is a reaction to life events. This kind of depression acts like a barometer to tell us when life is not meeting our basic needs. If you experience any of the following symptoms of burnout, listen to what they are trying to tell you:

1. Physical fatigue
2. Lack of concentration
3. Confusion
4. Sleeping less than or more than usual
5. Anxiety
6. Feeling overwhelmed
7. Outbursts of extreme anger or crying out of proportion to what is happening in the moment
8. Decrease in performance at work or home
9. Suicidal thoughts
10. Increase in negative self-talk
11. Mild paranoia, such as imagining that other people are judging you or angry with you when it is not the truth
12. Abuse or misuse of alcohol, drugs, or food to compensate for burnout

WHAT TO DO IF YOU ARE BURNED OUT

First, remember that you are being given a warning by your mind and body to wake up. This is the advantage that you have over the frog in the parable. You can feel the heat through any of the previously mentioned symptoms of burnout. Wiser with this knowledge, you can act to remove yourself from the boiling water. Here are some effective ways to turn down the heat on burnout.

1. Determine what has you feeling burned out: work, home, kids, partner, living above your means, too many responsibilities, money trouble, unresolved relationship issues with family or friends?
2. Go back to your pie chart exercise and see if there is an imbalance in your life. Make sure you are fulfilling your top priorities in some manner.

3. Review your values and make sure the thing that is causing burnout is worth the struggle.
4. If the source of your burnout is a fixed or necessary part of your life, then you may want to explore more effective management of this area. If it is something you can change, consider the pros and cons of letting it go.
5. If you have been given more responsibilities at work without an increase in pay, ask for a raise. If you have trouble being assertive, check out our chapter on assertiveness in Part 4.
6. Be sure to treat your mind and body with great care during this time. Eat healthfully, exercise, and find ways to nourish yourself.

Chapter 6

Giving as a Way of Life

KEITH'S STORY: *The Gift of Giving*

Keith came to the office complaining of depression, exhaustion, and a strong desire to drive his BMW off Flagstaff Mountain. He seemed to have it all—a successful law practice, a beautiful wife, three healthy children, financial security, good friends to golf and ski with—but all of this made him even more depressed. He was beginning to drink more heavily and felt distant from the life he had worked so hard to create. Something was missing, but what? One month into therapy, a wildfire ravaged the mountain neighborhood Keith lived in. His home was spared, but many of his neighbors lost everything. In the days and weeks after the fire, Keith marveled at how his neighbors had pulled together to help those who lost their homes. Keith was asked to help raise money for those who had no insurance. Pretty soon he and his family were helping with weekend house-raising parties. By the end of summer, Keith seemed like a different person. He was fit and tanned from his weekend volunteering. He spoke with a sense of wonder at how good it felt to be a part of the effort to help. He began to sparkle like a man who had found something he had been searching for for a very long time.

Did therapy help Keith? Probably. Did his service to others help? Without a doubt!

Somewhere along the way in our pursuit of the American dream we left behind our natural instincts for giving. We began to confuse quality of life with quantity of life in our search for meaning and happiness. Like Keith, many Americans feel that gnawing sense that something is missing, that the journey did not lead us to the goal we were promised. Some of us feel depleted at the end of the day, making the idea of giving seem like an impossible task.

Keith was lucky; life presented him with an opportunity to experience the joys of giving. Most of us do not have it thrust on us in this way. We need to find ways to open our hearts to the needs of others. Remember how good it felt the last time you opened a door for someone, performed a favor for a friend, or gave to someone in need. If remembering this brings a smile to your face or a warm feeling inside, then you probably are experiencing a positive benefit of your giving.

Why give? We believe that people are intended, both biologically and spiritually, to be there for one another. However, with the financial and emotional pressures of modern life, this has become difficult at best. We have become a society of rugged individualists looking out for ourselves and for our immediate families.

Studies show your health may depend on giving to others. Reports are now claiming that people who give live longer and are happier than people who do not. How could this be? For one thing, service is a feel-good behavior. It just feels good to give. Service to others is a wonderful way to rise out of your own angst and drop the misery for a while. If you are focused on someone else's challenges, it gives you an opportunity to gain a new perspective on your own life.

Service is at the core of most spiritual traditions and most addiction recovery programs. Many self-made millionaires attribute part of their success to giving 10 percent of their net income to others. It's amazing, but true, that when Ted Turner gave one third of his wealth to the United Nations, he not only ensured his continued success but also may have added years to his life. This is a man who knows the benefits of service, and we all profit from his generosity.

Often it seems that what is important to us has become a faint voice amidst the din of Wall Street marketing and our consumer-driven culture. "How did I get here?" becomes the lament of a generation of people whose good intentions have been slowly eroded from what had heart and meaning for them into the world of consume, consume, consume. "Buy this, buy into this, buy your way out of this" has become the siren call of mass media. One way to escape this particular pot of boiling water is by the simple act of giving. Norman MacEswan said it best in his simple stanza:

> *We make a living by what we get,*
> *but we make a life by what we give.*

STEPS TO BECOMING GENEROUS

1. Don't throw anything away until you are sure it cannot be used by someone else. Many charities take clothes, housewares, old paint, hardware, and used electronic equipment.
2. Give 10 percent of your earnings to charity.
3. Become a volunteer. Either formally at an agency or simply by helping shovel an elder's walk or going shopping for a shut-in.
4. Hug your loved ones every day, especially your children.
5. Give something back to this wonderful planet that supports all of us.
6. Reach out and bridge a disconnected relationship.
7. Adopt a pet from the Humane Society.
8. Pick up trash when you are out on a walk; even recycling one soda can could make a difference.

9. Consider supporting an environmental club or organization with your time, your money, or both.
10. Vote in all elections.
11. Consider becoming a foster parent or supporter of local child services organizations.
12. Make it a point to find new and creative ways to be there for your friends, family, and community.

TEACH YOUR CHILDREN WELL

Children can be taught to appreciate and enjoy giving at an early age. It is up to the adults in their lives to model this kind of behavior. Children learn by example. If you can show them the joys of giving, not simply the sacrifice, they will be curious about what you are doing. As they grow, they will learn more creative ways to help others. Unlike some of the teenagers in Plano, Texas, they will have meaningful lives as they approach adulthood; lives based not on acquisition but on sharing and helping the less fortunate.

Part 2

TURNING DOWN THE HEAT ON NEGATIVE THINKING

————

Every good thought you think is
contributing its share to the ultimate result
of your life.

Grenville Kleiser

There is an old parable that illustrates how reality can vary on the basis of perception. It is called the *Three Blind Men and the Elephant*. Once there were three blind men who came upon a circus in which there was an elephant. These men came from a part of the world where there were no elephants, so they were anxious to touch the great beast. The first blind man grabbed the trunk of the elephant and exclaimed, "Why it is like a mighty snake." The second blind man felt the elephant's hind leg and said, "No, no, you are wrong. It feels like a great oak tree." The last blind man grabbed hold of the elephant's tail and protested, "You are both wrong. This elephant is like a rope." Truth is, they were all right and all wrong. Describing the elephant was a matter of perception. So is life! ❧ There is a great deal of research that supports the conclusion that thoughts precede feelings and thereby create our moods, perceptions, and interpretations of daily events. This means each one of us has the ability to affect our mood, perception, and interpretation of our world simply by changing how we think. That's pretty exciting. It takes a commitment to listening more closely to our self-talk and learning a new way of thinking, one that creates an enthusiastic and positive interpretation of and reaction to life. This part of the book will give you the tools to begin this task.

Chapter 7

You Are What You Think,
So Think Carefully!

———

JAKE'S STORY: *A Higher Education*

Jake was sitting in his college history class when a teacher
burst into the room, screaming at Jake's professor and shoving
him. The argument grew more and more heated until the vis-
iting professor threatened harm and slammed the door on the
way out. An uneasy silence followed. Jake's professor told the
class to record quickly everything they had just witnessed.
Twenty students wrote twenty different accounts of the fight,
each sure of the truth of his or her story. But every version
added or subtracted from what really happened. Jake's professor wanted the students to see that history is recorded on the
basis of perceptions of reality that may have little to do with
the truth. It is a lesson Jake never forgot.

Have you ever had an experience like Jake's? If you have, you
are one of the lucky few who know there are seldom just two
sides to a story. There are as many sides as there are people interpreting. We each interpret events and come to unique con-
clusions. The conclusion is neither right nor wrong; it is simply
your reality based on your perceptions of the event. This section is about these perceptions, the reality these perceptions

create in your life, and how to change these perceptions to achieve a healthier attitude.

I THINK, THEREFORE I AM

Over two hundred years ago, French philosopher René Descartes emerged from pondering the meaning of existence to utter the famous phrase "I think, therefore I am." In some ways he was right. Many of us do not stop and listen long enough or hard enough to hear what it is we are thinking. Our thinking is how we interpret the world around us. If thinking creates how we interpret reality, it makes sense for us to pay a little more attention to what we are thinking and saying to ourselves.

THE ABC REACTION

Let's return to the parable of the elephant. How do we complete the picture so we know we are examining an elephant and not a snake, a tree, or a rope? The first step in determining the accuracy of your reaction is to discover how your reaction is generated. According to Albert Ellis, founder of Rational Emotive Therapy, reactions are generated in a three-step process called the ABC reaction.

One of the ways we maintain negative beliefs is through interpretation errors. Here is what we mean. Assume that every distressing situation has three elements: A is the stressor, which is the situation causing the distress; B is your interpretation of that situation; and C is your response to that stressor. For example, let's say you are driving to an appointment across town and get caught in stop-and-go traffic. You realize you will be late for your appointment and begin to talk to yourself. You may say, "I can't believe it. This is crazy. I'll never get anywhere at this rate. Why did I leave so late? How could I be so stupid?" You become tense, angry, and frustrated. Here's what actually happened.

1. You experienced an event (stop-and-go traffic), which is A.
2. You interpreted this event on the basis of old beliefs (and created negative self-talk), which is B.
3. This caused certain responses (anger, tension, and frustration), which are represented by C.

The ABC Reaction

Event   Interpretation   Response

Your responses were not caused by the event; they were caused by your negative self-talk. The good news is that even though you can't speed up the traffic, you *can* change your self-talk, which in turn will change your specific responses. In the traffic situation, regardless of your response, it appears you are going to be late. There may or may not be consequences for this, but your self-talk is not only unhelpful but increasing the discomfort of the situation.

We want you to realize that you reach a point in any situation when you can *choose* a path that will leave you angry, frustrated, and tense, or you can *choose* a path that will leave you connected, calm, and able to articulate accurately what happened. Because it is the negative responses that we want to address, we will focus on those for now.

We exhibit negative responses in three ways: behaviorally, physically, and emotionally. Behavioral responses might include overspending, drinking, and withdrawal. Physical responses might include muscle tension, fatigue, and headaches. And emotional responses might include frustration, fear, and anger. Now you will get a chance to chart the events to which you respond most negatively.

LIFE'S EVENTS AND YOUR RESPONSES

In the chart on page 64, we have listed a few life events and some ways to respond to them negatively.

LIFE EVENTS	STRESS RESPONSES		
	Behavioral	*Physical*	*Emotional*
Lost keys	Pacing	Muscle tension	Anxiety
	Slamming drawers	Sweating	Fear
Child acts out	Shouting	Clenching teeth	Anger
	Weeping	Headache	Sadness

In the following chart, first list the life events that you respond most negatively to on a behavioral, physical, or emotional level. Then, to the right of each life event, list the ways you might respond. The idea is to chart the level of negative response you are having to these events.

LIFE EVENTS	STRESS RESPONSES		
	Behavioral	*Physical*	*Emotional*
_____	_____	_____	_____
_____	_____	_____	_____
_____	_____	_____	_____
_____	_____	_____	_____
_____	_____	_____	_____
_____	_____	_____	_____
_____	_____	_____	_____
_____	_____	_____	_____
_____	_____	_____	_____
_____	_____	_____	_____
_____	_____	_____	_____
_____	_____	_____	_____
_____	_____	_____	_____
_____	_____	_____	_____
_____	_____	_____	_____

_____   _____   _____   _____
_____   _____   _____   _____
_____   _____   _____   _____
_____   _____   _____   _____
_____   _____   _____   _____
_____   _____   _____   _____

You now have a chart showing how your reactions create stress in your life. Your interpretations could be creating physical responses that may lead to illness or injury, or you may be creating emotional responses that influence the rest of your day or week. These emotional responses can spill over into other areas of your life and may surface inappropriately when you are with family or friends. Your actions may also be driven by your interpretations of events. You may find yourself drinking, overeating, or isolating. It is crucial that you understand how you are interpreting stressful events, especially when your interpretations rob you of physical and emotional health.

Chapter 8

Rehumanize Your Thinking

BILLY'S STORY: *The Need for Speed*

Billy was the top salesperson for a local sporting goods store. His success depended on a high-speed, charismatic personality and an increasing sales territory that took him up and down the Front Range of Colorado. As his territory grew, Billy began to drive more aggressively and compete with his route times from the previous week. He became increasingly upset with commuters who slowed him down, and he often screamed and shook his fist at these perceived enemies on the road.

One day, Billy came upon a long line of traffic moving at a snail's pace. After a few minutes of pacing at the back of the line, he floored the car and drove onto the shoulder. He derisively made note of the other drivers motioning him to stop as he picked up more speed. Billy finally came to the end of the line, literally and figuratively. He raced past the last car and braked too late to miss the overturned truck in the road.

Most of us can relate to Billy's need for speed and a clear road ahead. More and more, people are taking to the road like warriors. Some of us fight over every hard-earned second saved and every car passed, tallying them like the notches on the belt of a young gunfighter. We have catchy phrases to describe this new phenomenon: "Type A drivers" and "road rage." Yet what could be at the heart of this growing aggressiveness on our roads?

A client once shared an amusing analysis of aggressive driving. He believes our cars, often housed in our garages, become moving extensions of our private homes. We may be out in public, yet in the safety of our car we feel we are somehow unseen. Like children out of the watchful eye of parents, we act out. Notice some of the improprieties acted out in cars we would never think of doing in public. But, we *are* in public. We just don't see it that way.

We heard about Billy through a coworker of his who came to therapy in shock over his accident. Patti had been comparing routes and times with Billy for years and had treated their mutual need for speed as a big joke. Now, Patti was too terrified to drive. She reported having intense anxiety attacks at the thought of getting behind the steering wheel. She needed to work through her grief and anger over the accident and to look at driving a car in a very different light. Many of the following steps helped Patti overcome her fear and take driving more seriously and much more responsibly.

THE RULES OF THE ROAD

Here are some rules to consider before you drive one of these one-and-a-half-ton vehicles. You might even want to teach them to your kids.

1. Never drive angry.
2. Allow ample time for your trip.
3. Remind yourself, "I am sharing this road."
4. Keep calming tapes and music in your car for tense times.
5. If you have a car or cellular phone, use it only for emergencies; as the bumper sticker complains, "Hang up and drive!"

6. Don't use one of your hands to read, shave, or apply makeup. The steering wheel is designed for two hands, not one!

7. Try smiling when you drive; this simple facial expression can quickly change your mood.

8. Keep a tape recorder in the car for when you get stalled in traffic. Some great ideas have been born in traffic jams.

These ideas are behavioral in nature, but what about all the grumbling about those annoying drivers? Read on.

HUMANIZE YOUR SELF-TALK

Do you ever listen to your self-talk while driving? Maybe you are familiar with the following phrases.

"What an idiot."	*"Damned women drivers."*
"What a loser."	*"Old people shouldn't drive."*
"Hurry up!"	*"Damned men drivers."*
"What a jerk!"	*"Get outta my way!"*

Then there are the stories we make up about the other drivers. Maybe we imagine the slow driver ahead is trying to irritate us or the guy on our bumper is a homicidal maniac. Oftentimes we imagine the worst, because these drivers are competing with us. Here is a novel idea: Why not imagine the best about the other drivers?

There is a saying attributed to Buddha: You will not be punished *for* your anger, you will be punished *by* your anger. When you blow up at other people, you are the one who gets hurt—physically, emotionally, and spiritually. Sometimes anger can be a friend, warning you of danger, helping you set a necessary boundary, or allowing you to let go of built-up tension. But constant anger can build up in your body like a toxin, slowly eating away at your vitality and happiness. If you imagine the best about the other person, you have happier thoughts. Later, you will learn why positive thoughts are key to a happy life. For now, we offer you some steps to help you humanize the other people out there on the road.

Scenario 1

Imagine you are driving along the highway and a car comes up behind you. The driver starts flashing his lights, trying to convince you to pull into the right-hand lane. Your first inclination might be to judge him as a selfish man, endangering everyone in order to get to work on time. Here's how to humanize him. Imagine the best about him. He just found out his little girl is in the hospital and he is racing to see her. This is a thought that will make you want to pull over and help him out. He goes on by, you smile at your good deed and, surprise, no anger is left over.

Scenario 2

Imagine you are behind a young woman who is driving ten miles below the speed limit. You start self-talk about how she is driving you crazy on purpose. Now, imagine the best about her. She just started driving again after a horrible accident. You imagine she is afraid, so you are sure to give her plenty of room. You begin to relax and notice little things along the drive you never saw before. You smile because you just stopped yourself from sinking into a bad mood. You have humanized a potential enemy.

Scenario 3

You finally come upon the reason for the traffic jam you've been caught in for thirty minutes. Up ahead sits a young man in a broken-down old car, smack in the middle of the freeway. You begin to sneer at him and wonder why he drives that old piece of junk. You wish people like him would take the bus. Then you remember to imagine the best about him. You imagine he has fallen on hard times. This car is all he can afford and now it has failed him. You feel for his embarrassment at sitting there while all the commuters drive by and glare at him. As you pass him, you smile understandingly. You lose time but not your temper. You have humanized this fellow traveler.

After a time you will watch as this humanizing self-talk spills over into other areas of your life. When you imagine the best about others, you will feel happier and more at peace. Self-talk is often based on thinking errors—ways of thinking that are not grounded in reality—which usually create negative outcomes. In Chapter 10, we illustrate the seven most common thinking errors and how to recognize them. The next step, however, is to develop an inner guide, or teacher, to assist you in times of stress and indecision. You'll learn how to use this guide in the next chapter.

Chapter 9

Mindfulness: Fitness for the Brain

BRIAN'S STORY: *A Mind Like a Wild Horse*

Brian has a mind like a wild horse. It is in constant motion. He is the man you want on your team when playing Trivial Pursuit. His quick and agile mind has earned him two doctorates and a promising career as a research scientist. Brian loves his mind, except for one little problem: there is no off switch. When his mind moves rapid-fire through a technical issue, Brian is in heaven. However, when his mind moves with the same speed through his relationships, he quickly finds himself in quite a fix.

Brian came to therapy because his children complained they could not relate to him. After ten minutes of listening to him talk, it is easy to see why. Brian is full of facts, pithy observations, and theories about almost everything in his life. He makes almost no eye contact while he engages in a monologue about child development and the hazards of modern parenting. "Brian?" I ask, but he keeps on talking. "Brian?" I ask a little louder. He looks startled, as if he is not used to being interrupted. "Brian, what are you feeling right now?" "I feel like my children are unfair." "Brian, *unfair* is not a feeling. How do you feel about being treated unfairly?" Silence. Brian is mystified.

Sometimes we use the metaphor of a wild horse to teach clients the importance of disciplining the mind. What do trainers do with a wild horse? First, they know they have a one- to two-thousand-pound wild animal at the end of the rope. They have no illusions about forcing the horse to behave. Instead, the trainer will create rituals repeated again and again that create mental structures within the mind of the horse. A good trainer knows that repetition and precisely timed rewards can turn the most dangerous horse into a loyal friend.

We can do the same. First, we must realize that we have a wild horse in our heads. We must get rid of any illusion that we can force our minds to behave. Instead, we must develop repetitive rituals such as meditation, prayer, exercise, yoga, or repetition of a mantra that can create mental structures within our minds. Consider this: you wouldn't want to depend on an untrained wild horse to deliver you safely to your destination, nor should you depend on an untrained mind to guide you through your journey.

Brian's brilliant mind has tricked him into believing that thinking will get him anything he wants. His mind has been running the show for so long that he has trouble identifying feelings. Brian must learn to gain balance between what he thinks and how he feels. There is a good chance that feeling was not a safe behavior at some point in his life, so he overdeveloped his mind. Pretty soon his mind became his master. Brian needs to develop habits or rituals that can help him tame his mind. First, he needs to learn how to breathe deeply and consistently.

THE BELLY BREATH

Have you ever noticed that when children are frightened they tend to hold their breath and then take shallow breaths? As adults, we still use that old technique when we are tense, frightened, or upset. It's as though we think we see a monster in the bushes. The next thing we know, we feel anxious and tired, a clear sign we have stopped breathing properly.

Practicing proper breathing is a wonderful way to keep the mind engaged in a process that naturally slows it down. Proper breathing is essential to long life and good health. Improper breathing fails to cleanse the natural waste that builds up in the blood, leading to disease, anxiety, and fatigue. Breathing that is too shallow sends the mind into panic, because the mind is preparing for an emergency.

Belly breathing is a simple way to induce relaxation. Most of us tend to breathe only into our chest. Belly breathing takes the breath deeper, into our belly, and it is a much slower breath. This type of breathing is used in yoga, meditation, and the birthing process for expectant mothers.

How to Belly Breathe

Try stressful, improper breathing for a moment. Put your right hand on your chest and your left hand on your belly. Now, begin breathing fairly rapidly, taking air into the top part of your lungs only. Your left hand should not be moving at all. Take about seven or eight of these rapid breaths. Notice the effect on your body. Some people report that their heart speeds up, their muscles tighten, and they feel more stressed.

Now try these steps to a healthier way to breathe:

1. Place one hand on your chest and one hand on your belly. Just breathe normally at first.
2. Begin to inhale deeply through your nose and exhale through your mouth.
3. Picture your lungs like a bottle. When you breathe in through your nose fill the bottle from the bottom (your belly) to the top (your lungs).
4. Now exhale, picturing your lungs like a bottle emptying from the top (your lungs) to the bottom (your belly). Repeat steps 3 and 4 several times.

5. This time, as you exhale, focus on relaxing your body from the top of your head through your body, down to your toes. Take your time with this. Don't be in a hurry to inhale your next breath.

Go through these steps again, remembering to slow down as you exhale and to focus on your feelings of relaxation. Then pause for what Dr. Herbert Benson, author of *The Relaxation Response*, calls the relaxation point. The relaxation point happens just after you finish exhaling and are getting ready to inhale again. You can deepen your relaxation by noticing what happens at this point. Notice what your body feels like. Can you feel the warmth and heaviness in your limbs? Are you feeling more relaxed?

CREATING YOUR INNER GUIDE

The following guided meditation is one that you can record on a tape player and play back to yourself or have a friend read to you. Try playing your favorite calming music in the background as you recite the meditation into your tape recorder. The idea is to create a state of mindfulness that you can access at times of stress. This inner awareness or mindfulness will guide you through an event so your responses can become less destructive. Begin by talking yourself through the belly breath several times.

Guided Meditation

Now that you're more relaxed, start taking a personal inventory. Keep your eyes closed and begin by simply noticing your breath. Notice the air coming in and filling your chest and belly. Notice the air exiting your body and the relaxation deepening. (Pause)

Now, notice your toes, your feet. How are they contacting the floor? Are they relaxed? Tense? (Pause) Move up to your calves and knees. Feel your legs for a moment. What do you notice? Are your legs tense or relaxed? Can you feel all the areas of your lower legs? (Pause)

Now, scan your upper legs and your hips. What sensations do you no-tice? Are they relaxed or tense? Can you feel all these areas equally? Do any feel numb? (Pause)

Notice again your belly and chest. Are you still breathing in both these areas? Do you feel any tightness here? Now, notice your shoul-ders and arms. Are they relaxed? Or do they feel tense and stiff? Let your hands rest on the chair or on your lap. (Pause)

Notice your throat. Is it relaxed? Allow the tip of your tongue to rest at the back of your front teeth. Keep breathing slowly and steadily. (Pause) *Now move to your face and head. Do your eyes feel relaxed? Is your face relaxed or tense? Notice any tension you might be holding in your scalp.* (Pause)

Now, pull back and take note of your entire body. Where is there still tension? What part of your body draws your attention in this moment? (Pause) *What part of your body are you not noticing?* (Pause) *Take some time with this inventory.*

Now consider the following questions, respond in your mind, and think about your answers.

1. How is it that you were able to observe your body without using your eyes or your ears? Without even lifting a finger, you were able to survey your entire body's landscape. How?

2. Who or what was doing the observing? Obviously it was you, but what part of you?

The part of you that did the observing is a state of mindful-ness existing outside of your senses, outside of your experi-ences, and, most important, outside of your stress. You can call this part of you your guide, your awareness, or your inner voice. This inner guide can be activated and expanded to help you move through your day with a greater awareness of who and what is affecting you. This guide is a state of calm from which you can survey your life. With this awareness, you can identify and change the perceptions that create stress.

Now that you've discovered this guide, let's talk about how

you can use it. One way to use your guide is as a reporter. The bulk of any reporter's time is spent *watching*. They're observers by definition. They do not interfere with their subjects. A reporter works around the sidelines and *records* everything that is happening. This is one role your guide will play for you.

Your guide will see every circumstance as you see it. It will also see *you* in that circumstance. Your guide will observe your response to the circumstance and record it. Why do we want the guide along to do this recording? Simply because, as we rush through our days, we don't often take the time to see the forest for the trees. The guide is *you*. What it is doing is taking the time to step back from the hurriedness of your very real circumstances and showing you your own behavior. When you've taken this important step and recalled your situation, you can decide if the behavior you saw is the behavior you'd like to duplicate in the future or if it's not.

Let's go back to our traffic jam example. The jam, you may recall, is your stressor in this circumstance. In this example, your mind jumped to the negative self-talk ("I can't believe I left so late. This is crazy."). You interpreted the event as crazy and out of control. That is what generated the negativity. The self-talk inspired its own reaction—your stress response—and you became angry and frustrated.

Take a moment to go back and review your chart of life events and responses on pages 64–65. Where might a guide or an inner awareness have helped you respond more positively to life events? This is your point of control. You have complete control over how you interpret and respond to events. Let your guide help you interpret and respond in ways that make you feel more alive. If you are having trouble, do not despair. You might be caught in a thinking error, a kind of anti-guide that talks to you in negative ways. The next chapter begins with a case study that illustrates the damage a negative guide can cause.

Chapter 10

The Stressful Seven

———

DRAKE'S STORY: *I Am What I Am*

Drake came into therapy complaining about his lack of motivation and confidence in pursuing his graduate studies. His
voice, posture, and words reflected a man who did not have
much self-respect. "I am what I am," he muttered to no one
in particular. It begged a question, but I simply repeated his
statement back to him. He opened slightly at hearing the
phrase. "Yeah, a miserable failure, a worry for my parents . . .
incapable of finishing the simplest of tasks." Drake's self-talk
was brutal. I spoke with him about what I heard, and he
looked at me as if I were speaking Greek. Drake had become
so used to hearing the negativity that he saw nothing unusual
about my naming it. "If I let up on myself, I'll really fail," he
complained.

I used a metaphor of a track coach to explain the illogical
way he was talking to himself. "Imagine," I posed, "you are
about to run a race for your team. Before your warm-up,
your coach gives you a pep talk. 'Drake,' he says, 'you are a
miserable wretch and a failure. You probably won't even finish that race. So good luck and go get 'em!' " Drake began
to laugh. "That's ridiculous," he said. "How could I possibly
win after that?" "Well, Drake, isn't that how you talk to

79

yourself?" I asked. "How can you possibly complete your studies when your internal coach, or guide, talks to you in such destructive ways?" Now he really had something to think about!

The first step to understanding how we think in self-destructive ways is to study seven of the more common thinking errors made by most people. Thinking errors happen automatically. We misinterpret, then stress out about the misperceptions we created *ourselves*. Often, we don't really *hear* what we're saying to ourselves, but the results quickly show up as negative moods and/or physical tension.

Each of us makes thinking errors in our daily life. They become automatic, and sometimes hidden, forms of self-talk guaranteed to make our attempts to live a happy, contented life more difficult. It can be effective to approach these thinking errors in a lighthearted manner. The ability to laugh at the incredible ways we talk to ourselves is the first step in defusing thinking errors.

This section identifies what we believe to be the seven most common thinking errors. To help you remember each one clearly, we've assigned names you can easily remember. You've heard of the Dirty Dozen? We call this group the Stressful Seven. Each of these character descriptions begins with a case story, followed by a brief definition of the character. Finally, we demonstrate a few rational comebacks to use when dealing with each thinking error.

THE DRAMA QUEEN

RACHEL'S STORY: *My Life Is Ruined*

"I'll never teach again!" the young woman in the office cries out. "My career is ruined!" Rachel is in a panic. She arrived for her session thirty minutes early and is tied in knots by the time her appointment starts. Rachel teaches junior high school mathematics and was the Elder County Teacher of the Year in 1996.

Rachel is visibly upset and fidgets nervously in her chair as she explains what is bothering her. Last week she received the results of the school's peer evaluations. "According to them, I'm a fool and a charlatan." She hurriedly continues, "I can never show my face there again." The first thing Rachel needs to do is slow down and breathe. After about three breaths she launches into another diatribe about the ruins of her life. It's a good guess that Rachel has a thinking error.

About fifteen minutes into the session, Rachel calms down enough to explain more details of her ruined life. She had received a personally scathing review from one of her colleagues in the math department. "And the other reviews?" I ask. "Well they were okay, I guess." "How many were okay?" I ask. "Well," she replies sheepishly, "there were twenty-nine other reviews and they were all pretty positive." In the same breath she defends herself: "You wouldn't believe how mean-spirited this one teacher is."

Rachel is telling herself something about this situation that she believes to be true but is not grounded in reality. We call this thinking error the Drama Queen, because it involves making a melodrama out of a seemingly harmless incident. For instance, a bad review happens for Rachel, and in her view, her life is in ruins. It is likely that she employs this thinking error in other areas of her life. The Drama Queen is causing unnecessary stress by distorting reality to make a minor incident a catastrophe. Rachel's belief that her career is ruined is not logical. It doesn't make much sense. Yet this was the way she chose to interpret the situation. That interpretation creates her reality, and it's likely she will work hard to make it come true.

Rational Comebacks for the Drama Queen
The Drama Queen is a rather high-strung thinking error. It is a way of thinking that will create mountains out of any mole-

hill. When you feel your reaction and self-talk to a situation are beginning to escalate far beyond what is called for, try some of these rational comebacks. This is how a good guide would talk you through:

1. Take a few deep breaths.
2. There is nothing dangerous about this situation.
3. Take some time before you react to this.
4. Stay calm and focused.
5. This is a temporary problem so don't panic.

THE VICTIM/VILLAIN

SUSAN AND PETER'S STORY: *No One Understands Me!*

"You drive me crazy, Susan," Peter shouts at his wife, who is quietly sobbing at her husband's latest angry tirade. "You and all the people who push and push until I can't take it any more." Peter had another hard day at the auto dealership today. Hard days translated into verbal abuse aimed against his wife of ten years. This time Susan feels hopeless. After Peter leaves for work the next morning, she packs her belongings and moves in with a friend. When Peter arrives home, he goes wild, breaking dishes and picture frames in the house. "No one understands me," Peter screams. "Everyone is out to get me!"

Many types of domestic violence are common manifestations of the thinking error called the Victim/Villain. In this case, Susan has been raised to believe she has no right to set limits or to say no. She has no concept of assertiveness, and much of her life has been spent avoiding "rocking the boat."

Susan has perfected the art of avoiding conflict, which makes her the perfect match for a villain. The villain believes individuals do not have rights to personal boundaries. Victims and villains attract one another like magnets. Peter, who was abused as a child, feels justified in his role. He hardly sees himself as a villain. Susan, who watched her father berate her mother, feels this is her lot in life—to be a victim, that is, until she's had enough.

Susan cries to her friend, "I'll never get through this. No one understands me. Everyone will think I'm a bad wife." The words *never, no one,* and *everyone* are favorite words of both the victim and the villain. Notice how Peter used the same words to justify his actions.

The hapless victim loves words like *always, never, everyone, no one, all,* and *every.* The victim usually attaches these words to phrases like "I'm always the one to get hurt," "nobody likes me," and "it never goes right for me." The hurtful villain is simply the other side of the victim coin. The villain also loves words like *all, every,* and *everyone,* especially if they can be used in statements that reduce a group of people to stereotypes. The reason these two are connected is that they share a worldview that considers only black or white and right or wrong and pits me against you.

Rational Comebacks for the Victim / Villain

Every time you hear yourself say an all-or-nothing word or phrase like *everyone, no one, always, never, every time,* or *all,* throw up a red flag in your mind. It is time to call on your guide for a reality check. Your guide will help you temper these words by saying things like the following:

1. Is it really everyone who hates you? Who *does* like you?
2. Are you sure this always happens? When *doesn't* it happen?
3. Are all (police, women, jobs, minorities) this way or just this one?
4. Don't reduce your world to limiting words like these.
5. Remember the times things did go the way you wanted.

AUNT NINNY

ERIC'S STORY: *I Should Be Able to Rise Above This*

"It is simply not acceptable," complains Eric. "I must lose weight immediately!" Eric is a thirty-eight-year-old entrepreneur who runs a five-star restaurant in downtown Denver. He is an attractive and dangerously overweight man. His five-foot, ten-inch frame carries 300 pounds of weight, mostly distributed around his middle, a sure risk for the development of diabetes or heart disease.

Eric is a funny, warm gentleman with a generous heart for his friends and a strict agenda for himself. He continues his self-flagellation. "I look like a fat pig," he spits out. "It's not fair. I diet but keep gaining more weight. I should be losing. I should be able to rise above this." Eric is typical of many compulsive overeaters. Under the surface he is filled with shame about his failings, his abilities, and, most important, his weight problem.

Eric is an overweight perfectionist; his internal conflict is expressed in his well-tailored suit hung over his large frame. He is a walking contradiction, wearing his burdens like a suit of armor. Eric has a thinking error called Aunt Ninny. Notice how many times Eric says the word *should*. The thinking error called Aunt Ninny loves to "should" on you. This thinking error is a hard taskmaster and loves to keep Eric and others who share this error down.

The first line of treatment with Eric is to help him understand how his self-talk defeats his goals. Words and phrases like *should, must*, and *it's not fair* all work as weapons against his goal of losing weight. Fair or unfair really do not apply in the attainment of goals. Eric needs to understand that his pep talks are unreasonable, demanding, and self-humiliating.

Rational Comebacks for Aunt Ninny

This thinking error might appear in your self-talk as phrases such as "you should be working harder" or "you must do this, or else." Above all, this error induces guilt, so the next time you feel a twinge of guilt check your self-talk. Are you "shoulding" on yourself? When you hear words like these, use your guide to neutralize the negativity and turn down the heat on yourself. Try statements such as these:

1. Oops, there you go "shoulding" on yourself.
2. Instead of "should," what is it you really *want* to do.
3. You do the best you can and that is enough for now.
4. This guilt is not helping the situation.

THE PSYCHIC EXPERT

sophia's story: *A Mother Just Knows These Things*

"I know my children hate me!" Sophia mumbles as she sinks deeper into the couch. "I only want what's best for them, but they don't want me around." Tears well up as Sophia slumps forward in defeat. Sophia is a fifty-three-year-old Italian American mother of three grown children. Her youngest son is at the University of Denver, her middle daughter is married and has two children of her own, and her oldest daughter lives in Boston and works as an investment banker. Sophia came to therapy at the request of her husband, Rudy, who believes she is suffering from "empty nest" syndrome.

When I ask how she "knows" her children hate her, Sophia sits up and becomes animated. "Well," she exclaims, "Tony won't return my calls, Teresa doesn't invite me over, and Andrea doesn't come home anymore. It's obvious . . . they hate me!"

I ask Sophia if she has ever talked to her children about her concerns. "Why ask?" she answers. "A mother just knows these things." I ask if she might be afraid to ask her children.

She smiles knowingly. "No, no, no . . . you see, I know these kids better than they know themselves. They hate me and that is all there is to it."

Sophia has a thinking error. She is hiding behind the disguise of countless assumptions. She "knows" the truth, so why check it out with the kids? This is the thinking of the Psychic Expert. It is difficult for people who use this thinking error to be direct with others. They live their lives assuming how others think and feel, and they seldom check in with the "other" to see if their assumptions are true.

There are many issues for Sophia to work through as she adjusts to her children becoming adults. The first adjustment will be in her thinking. Sophia is given an assignment to help her break out of the Psychic Expert way of thinking and connect more deeply with her children as well as with others in her life. I suggested she sit down with each of her children and tell them what *she* thinks *they* think. She needs to begin having direct relationships with her children by expressing her fears aloud.

Sophia loves assumptions. She assumes she knows what others are thinking, feeling, and doing. Because she is so sure of the validity of her assumptions, she seldom checks them out. You see, Sophia loves to be in relationships. Unfortunately, most of her involvement in relationships happens in her own mind.

Rational Comebacks for the Psychic Expert

If you find this is an error you employ, practice assuming nothing for a day. Try to rely solely on what you know about a situation. If you hear the Psychic Expert deciding someone else's feelings, that's your cue to ask the person what you need to know. If you hear the Psychic Expert imagining the worst about a person, situation, or outcome, try imagining the best. Here are some rational comebacks for your guide to use when dealing with this thinking error:

1. You have no way of knowing if that is true.
2. Focus on what you are thinking right now, not on what you think someone else is thinking.
3. Remember this saying: "To assume makes an ass out of you and me."
4. Imagine they are thinking the best about you.
5. If you want help, be sure to ask for it.

THE BUSY BEE

TOM'S STORY: *It Was the Last Straw*

"Therapy is a waste of time," Tom hastily remarks, "but my supervisor insisted I talk to someone." This man is clearly irritated at having to sit with a complete stranger and explain why he slammed his fist through his office window yesterday. "Look, I know I snapped, but it's not that big of a deal. I'll pay for the window. I didn't hurt anyone." He sits on the edge of the couch, his leg vibrating up and down punctuating his rapid speech. "Look," he continues, "just give me a note or whatever to take to my boss and this can be all over in a matter of minutes."

Tom has a bandage around his right hand, covering the seventy-eight stitches the emergency room doctor sewed into his mangled hand last night. His body looks muscular and coiled like a spring ready to leap out at the world. "Well, what set you off?" I ask. "My damned coffee cup," he blurts out. "It spilled on a report I had been preparing all day. I just snapped. It was the last straw."

Tom is a typical Type A personality, living on adrenaline, speed, and perpetual motion. He chain-smokes, pumps countless cups of coffee into his body every day, drives like a madman, and puts himself to sleep with two cocktails every night. His wife has left him, his adult children cannot relate to him, and he has few close friends. It all seems quite normal to him.

The thinking error most closely associated with Type A behavior is the Busy Bee. You've probably seen these people in morning rush hour. They have a cell phone tucked under their ear, talk while they shave or apply lipstick, and gesture wildly at people obeying the speed limit (thereby slowing down his or her commute). Typically, accidents are the only events that snap a Type A out of this perpetual motion. For Tom, a mangled hand may not be enough of a wake-up call. He may have to suffer a heart attack or hurt another person before he wakes up to his destructive behavior.

The Busy Bee describes the little buzzing voice that tells Tom that his self-worth is based on his ability to perform. "You are only worth what you can accomplish in this world," it whispers to Tom. The Busy Bee loves activity—the more, the better. It revels in helping Tom get lost in the details of his life and seldom stops to see the bigger picture.

Rational Comebacks for the Busy Bee

The Busy Bee might be the little voice that starts in just as you've settled down with a good book. "What about the laundry?" it says. "Did you mail that letter today? Is the light on in the basement?" The Busy Bee can't tolerate rest or relaxation—it's a waste of time. Gotta stay busy. Early bird gets the worm, you know. You snooze, you lose. Here are some helpful responses for your guide to use to counter the constant chiding of the Busy Bee:

1. You are a human being, not a human doing.
2. Take a break.
3. Sometimes it is best to put off till tomorrow.
4. Relax, take some belly breaths, and then decide if this needs to be done right now.
5. When is the last time you had a break from all this doing?

THE WIZARD OF IF

ALLISON'S STORY: *If Only I Had . . .*

"If only I hadn't left Mary. If only we had tried to work it out. I bet I could be rich and famous like her." Allison is complaining about her failed relationship with Mary, a famous author who lives the high life in Beverly Hills. "I gave her the best years of my life, editing her proposals, rewriting her stories, giving her ideas. Now she's rich and I'm in the doghouse."

Allison is complaining bitterly about a relationship that ended over fifteen years ago. "What if I call Mary again?" she asks. "She always makes me feel better . . . for a while. Then I remember that little tart that came between us. If only I had been more careful not to let her too close to my relationship with Mary."

Allison suffers from the thinking error called the Wizard of If. Notice her wistful remarks, "what if" and "if only." Allison cannot move on in her life until she breaks the spell of the Wizard. The phrase *what if* leaves Allison hoping for a future outcome. The phrase *if only* leaves her stuck in a cycle of regret. Her therapy will focus on training her mind to replace the phrase *what if* with *I will* and the phrase *if only* with *the past is the past.*

The Wizard of If is the little voice that starts wondering what life would be like if. . . . What if I had married later in life? What if I had gone to college? What if I had bought into that real estate deal? This voice loves the past and would love you to live there permanently!

Sometimes The Wizard of If changes the wording a little and sighs, saying "if only." If only I had money. If only I were single. If only I were taller. You see, this voice wants you to wallow in a kind of eternal regret. What it avoids at all costs is the present, taking action, and, most of all, self-responsibility.

Rational Comebacks for the Wizard of If

When you hear these phrases, let your guide point out that you're living in the future or in the past. You can have the future you want only by taking action, not by pondering questions of "what if." You may not be able to undo things in your past, but you don't have to in order to change the present. Mistakes are okay; that's how we all learn. Here are some things your guide might say to you when the Wizard of If comes calling:

1. Instead of what *if*, how about what *now!*
2. Let this regret tell you what you want now.
3. Stay in the present moment.
4. Are you living a life based on your values here and now?
5. What are you willing to do to change things?

THE GREEN-EYED MONSTER

ERIN'S STORY: *Compare and Despair*

All her life, Erin has had a dream to play her music at Carnegie Hall. Unfortunately, Erin also has a chip on her shoulder the size of a barn door. "The music business sucks," Erin complains. "It's full of a bunch of no-talent, pretty boys who can barely carry a tune, not to mention play an instrument." She continues, "I would never sell my songs to some Nashville snake-oil salesman and then be paraded around like a prize heifer. No way, no how!"

Erin is a thirty-two-year-old musician who resides in a secluded mountain cabin and lives off her parents' monthly stipends. She hasn't performed publicly in years and spends her time spinning lonely ballads. She has little contact with the outside world and despises the business of music. How she expects to get to Carnegie Hall is a bit of a mystery at this point.

Erin is passionate and headstrong but suffers from a lack of direction and reality testing. Therapy will consist of harnessing her passion and her strong will into constructive ways of living. Her isolation and comparisons keep her in a continuous cycle of despair that must be broken if she is to rekindle her dream.

In therapy, Erin is encouraged to talk about her music and not compare it disdainfully to that of "others." Her comparisons leave her powerless and in a constant agitated depression. She needs to realize she cannot affect the music business unless she enters it with her own contributions. Under all the false bravado, Erin is terrified to try to break into the music business. She is a woman who has little experience with pushing against the world to see what impression she might leave. She seldom fails because she seldom tries anything risky.

Erin hides her fear of failure behind the thinking disorder called the Green-Eyed Monster. This is a way of thinking that keeps a person separate through the use of unfair comparisons with others, often leaving a person disempowered and bitter. Erin's criticism of others acts as a smoke screen to keep her from moving toward her dream.

Rational Comebacks for the Green-Eyed Monster

Most of you are familiar with the Green-Eyed Monster. It loves to convince you that your way of life is either better than or worse than other people's lives. It loves to make you green with jealousy and envy. Let your guide remind you that you might lose opportunities to make new friends when you make hasty comparisons that distance you from potential allies. If you catch yourself comparing, let your guide create a story that builds bridges instead of walls. It's a matter of finding common ground and letting go of comparisons that isolate you. Here are some things your guide might say when you hear yourself start comparing:

1. Everyone has strengths and weaknesses.
2. What are you going to do today to live up to your own strengths?
3. What are you going to do to improve your weaknesses?
4. Be curious about differences instead of judgmental about comparisons.
5. On some level, we are all the same.

YOUR FAVORITE THINKING ERRORS

Take a moment to evaluate which of the seven thinking errors apply to your life. The following chart illustrates a few examples of statements spoken and unspoken that may represent errors you make in certain situations.

Situation or Person	Words Used	Thinking Error
Fight with spouse	*You always do this!*	Victim/Villain
	You should be here for me.	Aunt Ninny
Late for work	*If only I had set the alarm.*	Wizard of If
	I wish I had the boss's life.	Green-Eyed Monster

Use the chart below to note when and with whom you use these or other errors. Remember the ways you can tell if a certain error is present. For instance, if you use words like *always, never, everyone, all the time,* or *no one,* you are using the Victim/Villain thinking error.

Situation or Person	Words Used	Thinking Error
_____	_____	_____
_____	_____	_____
_____	_____	_____

_____   _____   _____

_____   _____   _____

_____   _____   _____

_____   _____   _____

_____   _____   _____

CREATING RATIONAL COMEBACKS

The next step in changing negative responses into positive ones is to develop rational comebacks for each of the statements your thinking errors create. Remember that a rational comeback is a statement you say to yourself to neutralize the original negative statement. Here's what we mean.

Thinking Error	*Statement*	*Rational Comeback*
Victim/Villain	*He always does this!*	*He does this once in a while.*
Aunt Ninny	*You should be here for me.*	*I want you to be here for me.*
Wizard of If	*If only I had set the alarm.*	*Tonight I'll set the alarm.*
Green-Eyed Monster	*I wish I had the boss's life.*	*I want to try for a better job.*

Now, go back to your own list of thinking errors and develop some rational comebacks for them.

Thinking Error

_____

_____

_____

_____

Statement

_____

_____

_____

_____

Rational Comeback

_____

_____

_____

_____

Keep an ongoing journal of your thinking errors and rational comebacks. Pretty soon, the positive phrases you practice will become automatic. When this happens, those negative statements will seem false and awkward when they appear. Above all, have fun and be curious about how you talk to yourself.

Part 3

TURNING DOWN THE HEAT ON YOUR BODY

It is amazing to me that we can be
simultaneously completely preoccupied
with the appearance of our own body and
at the same time completely out of touch
with it as well.

Jon Kabat-Zinn

Imagine for a moment you are embarking on a cross-country adventure. You want to see as much as you can, enjoy a peaceful ride, and experience the best life has to offer. You begin to prepare for your great adventure, and first on your to-do list is transportation. You need to tune-up the vehicle, make sure it can withstand the long haul and get you safely where you want to go. You know this is the most important part of making the trip successful. So off you go! ❀ Now, imagine you are embarking on the only journey of your life, the one that starts with your birth and ends many decades later, when you are good and ready to leave. No one told you about the need to prepare for life, so you just take off in any direction. Halfway to somewhere, you run out of gas. Oops, forgot to check on the vehicle before you left. The vehicle? Your body, of course. ❀ How many times do you demand the impossible from a body filled with toxic substances, reduced to activities no greater than taking out the trash, and exhausted from needless stress and burnout. If you are like most people, you do this often. Yet you would most likely never leave on a road trip out of gas, badly in need of a tune-up, and running on bad gas from the cheapest station in town! This section is about turning the heat down on your body, whether it is practicing improved nutrition, getting off the couch, or learning to rest and relax after exertions. Life is an adventure; better to have reliable transportation!

Chapter 11

The Body Temple

———

RICK'S STORY: *I'm So Successful, It's Killing Me*

Rick is an old high school friend who was voted most likely to succeed in our senior class. Succeed he did! Rick bought an old electrical company his uncle used to run and turned it into a multimillion-dollar franchise. At our class reunion, I asked Rick how he was doing. Maybe because he knew I was a therapist, he dropped his big man on campus routine. "Truth be known . . . I'm so successful, it's killing me," he whispered. "I have high blood pressure from the demands of the franchise, gout from living the high life, and spastic colon from who knows what." "Maybe you need to get out of the business?" I posed. "Quit the business; what the hell would I do with myself? I have too much energy to just sit and vegetate or play golf." I wanted to say more, to shake him and tell him to wake up, but I drifted away as other classmates came over to congratulate Rick on his runaway success.

Success that is not tempered with rejuvenation, relaxation, and self-care can be a mixed blessing. Rick is not alone in paying a price for his rise to the top. High blood pressure and spastic colon are diseases associated with stress; gout, often referred to as the rich man's disease, is often coupled with body-numbing gluttony. Rick forgot to keep the transportation for his journey in good working condition. He placed his body under great strain without any regular tune-ups. Now he felt it was betraying him. In truth, he had betrayed himself. Our bodies are wired, somewhat like the frog in the water, to escape from sudden danger. In times of danger, our mind triggers an automatic response called "fight or flight."

FIGHT OR FLIGHT

One way stress tears down our body is by activating our natural fight-or-flight response. Fight or flight is adaptive today if you are fighting off a physical threat. Perhaps you have heard of the mother who lifted a truck off her child to save her. She needed the energy released by the fight-or-flight response. Usually, these are rare moments in our lives. The trouble begins when we use fight or flight to respond to social situations that are much less dangerous.

Let's see how this instinctual response works. Say you're on your way to an important meeting. Ahead, you see two miles of taillights blinking in unison. Traffic comes to a complete stop. You are going to be late. First you may say, "Oh, no!" (This is your mind responding.) When you say this, your brain becomes aware of an emergency.

Your brain stimulates the entire nervous system and your adrenal glands. Within seconds, your muscles are tense and ready for action. Next, you start to breathe faster, starting with that first gasp of recognition. Your windpipe opens wider to let in more oxygen. Your heart starts beating fast and loud as it pumps fuel and oxygen to your brain so you can think fast about how to react.

Next, your heart pumps fuel to your big muscles so you can run fast or fight well. Your brain decides to shut down nonessential areas of your body, so it shuts off vessels leading to your stomach, hands, and feet. Your stomach gets tight, you feel nauseous, and your hands and feet become cold. Your blood pressure skyrockets. Glucose and fat are rocketed into your bloodstream to give you quick energy for the emergency. You start sweating to release the heat generated by all this activity. You are now ready either to defend yourself (fight) or to run away (flight). ALL THIS ACTIVITY TOOK SIX SEC-ONDS—ONLY SIX SECONDS! And this was only a re-sponse to a traffic jam!

Here is the point: The fight-or-flight response does not help you deal with the kids. It does not help you pay your bills or cope with an irrational boss or an unexpected visit. It does not help you win an argument with your spouse or get you to an appointment any faster.

What it does, if you don't learn to turn it off when you want to, is make you sick. By now you have learned ways to inter-cept the errors in thinking that lead to stress. This section will teach you how to create a resilient body able to handle the stress that is not under your control. Why get a handle on the fight-or-flight response? If your don't, this response could change your life direction to a downward spiral ending in ill-ness, addiction, and/or impaired mental health.

We are fortunate our bodies are programmed with this re-sponse. It is the reason our species has managed to survive! There may still be occasions when your survival depends on this response. For instance, if you are being physically threat-ened, you will need the energy burst to run away or fight. However, if triggered too often, the response can have danger-ous effects. What are the health risks for this response? Let's take a look.

STRESS AND ILLNESS

You may know about the part cholesterol plays in heart disease. But did you know that each time you engage your fight-or-flight response you might be increasing your serum cholesterol level by as much as 60 percent? A fascinating study was carried out by researchers looking at the effects of stress on the cholesterol levels of accountants as the April 15th tax deadline approached. They found that cholesterol levels shot up during this time and began to come back down after April 15th. Sometimes the level did not return to normal after repeated stress.

Remember how your brain began to cut off the blood supply to your stomach? Gastroenterologists are well aware of the role this plays in digestive tract disorders. Accumulated stress can lead to gastritis, stomach and duodenal ulcers, ulcerative colitis, diarrhea, constipation, and gas pain.

Do you ever feel fatigued at the end of your day? Do you know that fatigue is rarely caused by physically tiring work? Most of us are tired because our stress tightens up our muscles and, over time, we become fatigued. This accumulated tension can also cause tension or migraine headaches. Accumulated muscle tension can lead to physical pain in our muscles and joints. Back pain, one of the most common problems presented in doctors' offices, is often due to accumulated tension from stress.

Here's the list so far. Your stress may cause high blood pressure, heart disease, gastritis, stomach and duodenal ulcers, ulcerative colitis, diarrhea, constipation, gas pain, fatigue, aching muscles and joints, back pain, and headaches. Add to this list skin disorders, breathing and lung problems, and biochemical changes in your moods.

Here's the kicker: The worst effects of stress are found in the immune system. The strength of the immune system determines how we deal with infections, colds, the flu, and more serious disorders such as cancer and AIDS. This is not to say that stress causes cancer but that our ability to fight cancer is weakened when we are under stress. Many scientists believe we have cancer cells in our bodies at all times. Researchers have discovered that the body's production of its own cancer-fighting cells, such as T lymphocytes, is inhibited by chronic stress. A healthy immune system has the ability to fight these cells. A stressed system does not.

The American Academy of Physicians estimates that three fourths of visits to doctors' offices are stress related. The last time you visited the doctor, three out of every four people in the waiting room with you were there because they did not know how to turn off the fight-or-flight response.

We hope this chapter has put a little healthy fear into you. Our bodies are amazing, resilient things of beauty and wonder. But if we ignore or abuse them, they begin to deteriorate. The following chapters provide you with simple approaches to get your relationship with your body back on track. These simple approaches focus on the areas of nutrition, fitness, brain care, and relaxation.

Chapter 12

Nutrition for a Quality Life

TAYLOR AND JESSICA'S STORY: *What's Eating You?*

Taylor and Jessica came to therapy because they were starting to hate their life together. Pretty strong words for newlyweds. They had been in couples counseling for about a month when the issue of food came up, quite humorously. Jessica was busy listing the complaints of the week against Taylor when he began to laugh. "Good grief, Jessica, eat an energy bar and chill out!" he admonished. Jessica's face turned beet-red, and she began to clench her fists. It was time for a couple's time-out. I requested they both be silent for a moment and only respond to my questions. I waited a few minutes for them to calm down before beginning my query.

"Taylor, what was the comment on energy bars about?" I asked. "Oh, she forgets to eat sometimes and turns into a real terror. Even her friends are hip to her mood swings," he replied. By now, Jessica was fuming. "Okay, Jessica, what about Taylor's comment makes you so angry?" I inquired. She paused and began to weep. "I feel like I'm on this treadmill with Taylor. We hike, we run, we go to work, we have really physical sex, and then we pass out from exhaustion. How I am supposed to remember to eat?" she complained. "Oh, come on," Taylor answered. "It's not like we starve ourselves.

We just stopped and had an espresso and bagel before therapy.""What about dinner?" I asked. It was 8 P.M. on a week-
night and neither one had had dinner or much of a lunch.
Taylor seemed to respond to lack of food by becoming more
hyper and then crashing over the weekend. Jessica was hypo-
glycemic and experienced intense mood swings when she
went without food. No wonder they hated their life together;
they were both literally too hungry to enjoy themselves.

This couple represents a growing throng of eat-on-the-run
Americans. We grab something here and there, seldom considering what we are putting into our mouths, and rarely sit
down at a table to have a meal. Fast-food chains are responding
by creating foods we can eat with one hand, leaving the other
free to drive the car. Car designers respond by installing cup
holders in every new car. Coffee shops respond with drive-
through windows. What in the world are we doing to our
bodies?

If your body is your transportation, then food is its fuel. Do
you know what happens when you put sugar in a gas tank? It
gunks up and destroys the engine. Funny thing, the same thing
happens when you throw sugar, fatty foods, coffee, alcohol, and
drugs into *your* tank. It may take years, but eventually your engine—your heart—will gunk up and begin to deteriorate.

What is healthy nutrition? Most people groan when they
hear the words *diet* and *exercise*. We don't believe in diets, nor
do we believe in no-pain, no-gain exercise. We do believe in
balanced nutrition and lifelong fitness. In this section, you will
learn some basic guidelines for proper nutrition, fitness, and
relaxation. Let's start with nutrition and why it does not mean
diet!

More than 90 percent of all diets fail because they are often
quick fixes that do not promote lasting lifestyle changes. This is
why we use the word nutrition. Why are nutritional changes
best? Eating right and living right are deeply interrelated. If
you use the principles you have learned in this book to turn

down the heat on your relationships, thinking, and behavior, you will find you want to eat in a way that gives you energy for changes. If you eat in a healthier way, you will find yourself developing other good habits that move you naturally in a healthier direction.

Nutrition books fill the bookstores. Ask around and see what is working for other people in your life. There are many nutritional ideas. You simply need to find the right program for you. Again, look for commonsense nutrition, not diet extremes or promises of quick fixes. Lifestyle changes take time and moderation. These are the changes that will last long after fad diets have left people heavier and less fit than before they started dieting.

MODERATE EATING

If you have health concerns, consult a physician or nutritionist to determine the best nutritional plan for you. Here are some key points for eating in a healthier way:

1. Eat five servings of fruits and vegetables each day. This is the single most important thing you can do to feel healthier!
2. Try different combinations of carbohydrates, protein, and fat to see what works best for you. We have included a list of diverse books in our bibliography. Have fun discovering a new way of eating, as you would in experiencing a trip to a new country.
3. Make your kitchen a healthier place. Nutritional changes start at home. Dr. Andrew Weil lists steps to transform your kitchen into a place of healthy eating in his book *Spontaneous Healing.* For instance, changing your use of oils to olive oil and canola oil will reduce your intake of the harmful fats found in butter and margarine.
4. Practice moderation, not deprivation, in any lifestyle change, especially nutrition.

5. Create a healthy setting for your meals by eating at your dining table. Don't choose mealtime to have business or house meetings or resolve conflicts. Make it a nourishing, peaceful setting.

6. *Do not watch television while you eat!* You will eat more food, of poorer quality, and with less enjoyment if you eat while you "zone out" in front of your TV.

7. Stay aware when you're eating: Slow down, think about it, and focus on the joy of eating, not the goal of finishing so you can rush to the next thing.

8. Your body is your temple, so what goes into a temple? Fast food or fruits and vegetables? The sad truth is we often put better fuel in our cars than in our bodies.

9. If your eating is out of control, seek professional help. Nothing is as important as treating your body well.

10. Drink at least eight glasses of water each and every day.

11. Eliminate or limit your intake of alcohol.

12. Find a role model, someone who simply "glows" with good health and vibrancy. Ask how he or she does it.

Chapter 13

Fitness for a Quality Life

_____

ROGER'S STORY: *Gone to Seed*

Roger used to be an excellent basketball player. He was right guard on his high school and college teams and made all-American his senior year at the university. During those years he ate what he wanted, partied when he wanted, and reveled in his identity as a jock. Roger tells his sports stories with a gleam in his eye. I can almost see him on a fast break tearing down the court. Then I look at this thirty-five-year-old man and marvel that he was ever an athlete at all. Roger has gone to seed. He stopped working out after college, still ate what he wanted, and gained about thirty pounds. He came to therapy because he was thinking of having an affair with a colleague at work. Trouble is, Roger has a wife and two kids at home.

I noticed that when Roger spoke about this potential affair, he had that same gleam in his eyes. I asked what he saw in her and he explained, "Emily is a babe. She has a terrific body, she's full of energy, and she seems to be attracted to me!" He marveled at the last part. "Why do you seem so surprised that she finds you attractive, Roger?" I asked. He wasn't sure at first. In the following weeks, Roger opened up about his distaste at aging and losing the youthful athlete he once was.

He never formed an identity after college he felt as good about as that of a basketball player. Enter Emily, full of youthful energy and good looks. It was just what his ego needed but not worth the risk of losing his family.

Roger was a faithful husband and able to control his impulse to have an affair. This gave him the opportunity to look at what was missing in his life that made Emily seem so appealing. One thing missing was his love and enthusiasm for his body. He seemed disappointed that his body was aging and not able to stay muscular with no effort on his part. He scoffed at suggestions to find that part of himself again. He claimed sports were for kids, not old men like him. So he sat on his couch all weekend watching college kids play sports. Each year brought a new flock of freshman standouts, more reasons to despair his aging process.

Roger represents a burgeoning group of ex-athletes who grudgingly become spectators and forget to take care of their precious bodies. There is a polarization in this country between people who give up on self-care and exercise fanatics. This part of our book is not for fanatics, extreme athletes, or body perfectionists. This section is a call to the rest of us who are sitting like couch potatoes watching other people enjoy wonderfully strong and supple bodies. Whether it is spectator sports, television zoning out, or that we are just too busy to notice, we are becoming a rather unfit, undernourished country. And there really is no excuse for it. The demands of this century, the speed at which we move, and the stress that we create all demand more and more resilient bodies. Yet our overall fitness levels have headed south.

The benefits of regular exercise are vast: reduced risk of bone disease and heart disease, lower blood pressure, improved cholesterol levels, lower body weight, improved insulin sensitivity, lower blood sugar, lower risk of developing diabetes, improved mood, raised serotonin levels, and higher self-esteem. And *it helps reduce stress!*

For the vast majority of Americans who do not exercise regularly, and this is most Americans, the idea of exercise is unpleasant. Often people have images of sweaty gyms filled with sculpted athletes moving about in the latest spandex wear. If you like that, great. If you're intimidated or turned off by this picture, please know this represents a tiny portion of people who exercise regularly.

Guess what the fastest growing exercise is in this country? It's walking! Simply putting one foot in front of the other for about thirty minutes a day. As a matter of fact, if you start to walk thirty minutes a day and make no other nutritional or fitness changes, you can lose up to twenty-one pounds in a year.

MODERATE FITNESS

Walking may not be your choice. Your options are endless. To find what's right for you, follow these steps:

1. Pick a fun activity. If it's not fun, chances are you won't do it for long.
2. Learn to exercise properly so you don't increase your physical stress and cause injury.
3. Always, always, stretch before you exercise! Warm up aerobically for about five to ten minutes and then stretch for fifteen to thirty minutes.
4. Find people to exercise with, and schedule it into your day. It's just as important as all those other activities in your schedule.
5. Exercise early in the day. Research shows that people who exercise in the morning have a much greater chance of maintaining their exercise program than afternoon or evening exercisers.
6. Begin your activity gradually. Don't overdo it. Exercise can be fun and should not be torture.

7. Reinforce and reward yourself for any successes, however small. Treat yourself to a movie, a healthy meal out, a new book, new clothes in a smaller size, and so forth.
8. Post encouraging reminders, such as "keep it up" or "you're doing great" in places where you will spot them.
9. Use images of yourself to stay motivated. See yourself healthier, fitter, and/or thinner.
10. Consider a few more options: housecleaning, raking, weeding, and washing your car. All these activities exercise your body.
11. As you age, add weight-bearing exercise, such as walking, to your fitness program. Studies show training with simple hand weights can also create increased strength and endurance for elders.
12. Again, find a role model, someone whose fitness and endurance you admire and seek to emulate.

FITNESS DISGUISED AS EVERYDAY LIFE

Here are some tips on how to incorporate fitness into your life without creating any kind of exercise regimen. There are many opportunities to stay fit in the ordinary routines of our lives.

1. Use the stairs instead of the escalator or elevator whenever possible. If there are too many flights, try climbing stairs for a bit and then take the elevator.
2. Walk instead of ride whenever possible. If you have to ride, park the car away from your destination and walk the rest of the way. If you are using public transportation, get off one or two stops before your destination and walk the rest of the way.
3. Stand when you normally might sit.
4. Take a walk as a form of work break.
5. Do not order food in; instead, walk to get it yourself.
6. When you need something from the store, walk there instead of driving.

7. When you walk your dog, make your walks longer.
8. At home, use the upstairs bathroom when you are downstairs and vice versa.
9. When the phone rings, answer the one farthest away from where you are.
10. At work, use a washroom farther away from your desk than the one you currently use.

Chapter 14

Brain Food

JEFF'S STORY: *The Yuppie Diet*

Jeff came into therapy complaining of depression and fatigue. Part of his intake included an assessment of the state of his nutrition. When clients name symptoms of depression, it is always a good idea to check their nutritional and fitness habits. I looked at Jeff's intake and raised my eyebrows over his nutrition. "Jeff," I asked, "what in the world kind of diet is this?" He chuckled and answered, "Come on, you must know it's the yuppie diet. Coffee in the morning, Snickers bar for lunch, a burger and two glasses of wine before bedtime." "Did you ever consider this unusual diet may be contributing to your depression?" I queried. "Diet and depression," Jeff balked. "What does one possibly have to do with the other?"

In the last chapter we discussed why good nutrition is essential for a healthy body. It is also a cornerstone of a healthy brain. Improper nutrition can severely affect brain functioning and lead to depression, anxiety, and mood swings. Poor nutrition can create surges of insulin overload and depletion, which leave the brain lurching in and out of hunger. A hungry brain is not a pretty thing to behold. If you deprive your brain of essential nutrients, it will respond with extremes of functioning.

This can create havoc with your thinking and coping skills. Yet when we feel stressed, we often react by consuming substances that make the stress increase.

POURING GASOLINE ON THE FIRE

Some people eat, smoke, drink, spend money, or misuse drugs when under stress. Why do we do this? When we try to cope with modern stressors by smoking, overeating, drinking, spending money, and misusing drugs, we are making matters worse by adding to our stress. When we feel the increased stress, we respond by adding more food, alcohol, cigarettes, and drugs. True, we may feel better at first, because all of these substances change our moods for a short time, but we are actually stressing our immune systems further. If we keep up these temporary fixes, it becomes like throwing gasoline on a fire in an attempt to put it out!

Why do we crave cigarettes, alcohol, sugar, chocolate, or caffeine? There is a great deal of research out today that supports the notion that we ingest many of these substances in a misguided attempt to balance the biochemistry of our brains, a balance seriously disrupted by the harried lifestyles of the twentieth century. The most influential of the chemicals in the brain is serotonin, which functions as a neurotransmitter, conveying messages from cell to cell throughout the central nervous system.

Serotonin is influential in regulating body temperature, blood pressure, immunity, pain, blood clotting, digestion, body rhythms, and sleep patterns. Serotonin inhibits many of our more primitive behaviors such as aggression, overeating, sexual compulsivity, and addictions to alcohol and drugs. It also comforts the body and functions as an important stress reducer and tolerator. Sounds pretty important, yes?

Well, it is. And most of us are deficient in this essential brain chemical. Fortunately, there are many ways to increase serotonin levels, both naturally and with prescription medication.

The most effective ways to increase your serotonin level are:

1. Proper nutrition
2. Exercise
3. Sleep hygiene
4. Light therapy
5. Relaxation and rest
6. Medication

PROPER NUTRITION

Our brains are sustained by the glucose in our bodies; therefore, maintaining balanced supplies of glucose is essential to having a healthy brain. Proper nutrition is the best way of maintaining this balance. It is best to avoid substances that spike the glucose in the body. These are things like candy bars, foods with high concentrations of sugar, high-fructose juices, and some carbohydrates. Most of us have experienced that rush that comes after we eat a food with lots of sugar. We may become giddy, hyperactive, or elated. About an hour later, we are ready for a nap.

This swing represents a trauma that your body is experiencing as it tries to process too much sugar. The sugar you ingested raises your insulin level and signals your brain to cut back on insulin production. Then when the sugar quickly leaves your body, the insulin is secreting at a much lower level and you become fatigued. Your brain is experiencing a big swing in energy, which affects your mood, your energy, and your thinking.

Sugar is in a great many processed foods. It can be a wonderful treat, but in large quantities or eaten frequently it can play havoc with your brain and other organs. Remember the basics of good nutrition, and limit your intake of sugar whether it is in candy, alcohol, or processed foods. Watch especially for foods that advertise themselves to be low fat. Many of these foods contain far more sugar than your body can process and just as many calories, if not more, than higher fat products.

EXERCISE

Exercise is a natural way of increasing the levels of brain chemicals that leave you feeling happier and more content. It is a cornerstone of the treatment plan for clients who are suffering from depression.

SLEEP HYGIENE

Sleep deprivation has been shown to significantly decrease serotonin levels in the brain. There are levels to our sleep. Researchers have found that Level 4 sleep, which is described as coma-like, is essential for maintaining brain health. Alcohol taken in the evenings can deprive one of Level 4 sleep. Lack of Level 4 sleep affects the part of the brain that acts like a tuning fork, the medulla. This area will become hypersensitive and render us unable to deal with everyday pressures.

Buysee and Reynold's book *Insomnia* recommends a set of rules for better sleep:

Twelve Rules for Better Sleep

1. Sleep only as much as needed to feel refreshed during the following day. Restricting time in bed enhances sleep, and excessively long times in bed lead to fragmented and shallow sleep.
2. Get up at the same time each day, seven days a week. Regular wake-up times lead to regular bedtimes.
3. Exercise on a regular basis. A steady daily amount of exercise in the morning or afternoon deepens sleep.
4. Insulate your room against sound or nocturnal light.

5. Keep your room temperature cool—not too hot or too cold.
6. Both hunger and excessive fullness can disturb sleep. Eating a light snack before bedtime may help sleep.
7. Avoid excessive liquids in the evening to minimize the need for nighttime trips to the bathroom.
8. Avoid caffeinated beverages (coffee, tea, colas) after 2 P.M.
9. Avoid tobacco as it disturbs sleep.
10. Avoid alcohol, especially in the evening.
11. If you feel frustrated or angry about not falling asleep, get out of bed, go to a different room, and do something different. We fall asleep by *not trying.*
12. If you find yourself looking at the clock at night, turn it so that you cannot see it, or cover it up.

In addition to following these rules, try including a fifteen- to twenty-minute nap in your day. Be sure not to exceed twenty minutes or you may feel more tired when you awaken. Catnaps are great for refreshing the mind and body.

LIGHT THERAPY

Before the advent of electric lights, we derived most of our light exposure from the sun. Now, we live inside most of the day under indirect lights that are a poor substitute for the sun's healing powers. For instance, a well-lit office emits approximately five hundred lux (one lux equaling the brightness of one candle flame). A sunny day, on the other hand, offers 50,000 to 100,000 lux! Even a cloudy day can measure several thousand lux compared to the meager five hundred lux of an office. In short, we are light starved, and exposure to light is key in maintaining healthy levels of serotonin. Studies of seasonal affective disorder (SAD) have shown that increased exposure to light greatly improves the health of SAD sufferers. Here are some ways to increase your exposure to light:

1. Spend forty-five minutes every day outside, preferably without sunglasses. You do not have to be in direct sunlight to benefit.
2. If mornings are a rough time, consider investing in a dawn simulator. This simple device connects to your lamp and slowly turns the light on each morning to simulate sunrise.
3. If you have a work schedule that keeps you indoors, consider investing in a light panel that will sit on your desk and give you the necessary lux you need each day.
4. If you suffer from SAD, a light visor that keeps a steady flow of light coming into your eyes may be beneficial.

RELAXATION AND REST

Have you ever heard yourself say, "I just don't have time to rest"? For many of us, relaxation is equated with sleep. But there is a marked difference between these two ways to rejuvenate your mind and body. We talked about how important sleep is, but what about relaxation?

Relaxation is vital to resting your overworked mind. It can also help boost levels of melatonin in your body. Why is melatonin important? Melatonin regulates the natural rhythms of your body so you know when to sleep. It also inhibits the fight-or-flight response, so you don't overreact to everyday pressures, and it stimulates the parasympathetic nervous system, associated with calming you down. Melatonin is also believed to neutralize free radicals. Free radicals are generally thought to contribute to conditions such as cancer, heart disease, and arthritis. Sounds like a pretty important chemical, doesn't it!

Studies of meditators have shown them to have increased levels of melatonin, indicating that meditation or prayer increases melatonin in the body. This could be the reason for the calm and relaxed feeling that often occurs in people who meditate regularly. Certainly, all of us have had the experience of sitting quietly in tranquil settings and feeling a sense of inner calm and peace. It could be we are experiencing raised levels of melatonin.

Proper Breathing and Relaxation

The way you breathe affects the health of your body, the state of your emotions, and the clear functioning of your mind. Most of us have learned to take air only into our lungs and very little makes its way to our abdomen. Breathing into the belly is essential for relaxation, calm, and clarity.

The True Meaning of Vacation

Another way to reduce stress is to take a vacation. But have you ever looked forward to a vacation and then found it impossible to relax or that you end up sick? What's worse, you have to come back. If you come home on a Sunday night, by Monday afternoon it feels as if you never left. And here's the kicker. Researchers have found that many vacations produce their own stress, rather than reducing accumulated stress. There is evidence that long weekend vacations are more rejuvenating and less stressful than the traditional one- to two-week vacations. The best part about long weekends is that you can take more of them, more often. This also reduces the chance that illness, accident, or delays in travel will ruin your vacation time.

To take a vacation simply means to vacate, or empty, oneself. This can be done every day with meditation. There is a story about a reporter who asked the great pacifist Gandhi when he had time to take a vacation. He replied, "I am always on vacation." He had learned to live a life that was so calm and steady that every day felt like a vacation.

MEDICATION

Many people who suffer from depression are helped by the new generation of antidepressants. Fortunately, the stigma of taking this medication is beginning to diminish. There is talk of a new medication without the side effects of antidepressants that will revolutionize the treatment of depression in the near future. We believe medication can be very helpful for people who have trouble stringing enough good days together to change habits that intensify their depression. Medication can be the boost they need to change their lives. However, for many people medication becomes more than a short-term solution. If they do not make the necessary changes outlined in this book, they may be dependent on the medication all of their lives.

Chapter 15

Body Image

CHRIS'S STORY: *The Mirror Does Lie*

Chris came to therapy to figure out why she could not lose weight no matter how much she starved herself and exercised her body. The woman who entered the room was a stunning blonde, tall and physically fit. She appeared to have the body of a professional athlete. In our work with clients with eating disorders, we were used to this incongruency between how clients reported seeing their bodies and how they actually looked. Yet it is still amazing when a young, beautiful, and lithe woman walks into the office professing to be overweight and unattractive. How could this distortion have happened?

In Chris's case it was part of family messages, such as "you can never be too rich or too thin," that were embedded in her mind and self-talk. It is also a cultural phenomenon—an advertising-driven image of what it is to have the "perfect" body (even though many models' bodies are airbrushed to make them look unreasonably thin or perfectly sculpted). Chris hung out with young adults who rock-climbed the mountains around Boulder. Most of these friends had extremely low body fat, rock-hard muscles, and a competitiveness that verged on obsession.

We conduct our therapy practices in the fitness mecca of Boulder, Colorado, an outdoor paradise that is home to countless sports enthusiasts and world-class athletes. We are familiar, therefore, with the alternate side of fitness and beauty: eating disorders, exercise-bulimia (the use of exercise to purge the body of food in an unhealthy manner), and sports therapies to treat increasing numbers of stress injuries. Some of us are becoming Type A exercisers and dieters, a group that is becoming known as *extreme athletes*.

ADVERTISING AND BODY IMAGE

On September 8, 1998, *CBS Nightly News* reported that the average American consumer sees between fifteen hundred and three thousand advertising commercials each day. The field of eating disorder treatment has long recognized the tremendous impact of much of advertising on the body image of young women. Years ago, one female who modeled adult fashions was found to be only twelve years old. She had a preadolescent body shape without hips, breasts, or the other natural curves of a woman. Recently, fashion designers started parading washed out–looking teenagers in baggy clothes. Critics referred to this as the "heroin" look. Now *there's* a role model for young adults—bodies that appear as if they are wasted by drugs! Today, photography brings us the airbrushed model: one who exists only on the magazine pages.

The first step in changing a negative body image is to become aware of the false and unrealistic images of beauty that are spoon-fed to us by the advertising industry. Armed with this awareness and a little healthy indignation, we can begin to understand the forces at work to make many of us dissatisfied with our bodies. Following are key steps to take to begin to change how you view your body.

STEPS TO AN IMPROVED BODY IMAGE
Enjoy Your Body

Your body is a marvelous creation of billions of cells organized in a unique way that represents you and you alone. Why spend time comparing when there is no comparison? You can certainly try to bend it and shape it into some idealized body, but it may take a lot of time and effort, and it may even shorten your life in the process. You can get tanned, tucked, lifted, and lasered in order to satisfy the demands of beauty. That is your choice. However, at times, outside pressure can make you feel that the choice is not yours to make.

Improve Your Personal Body Image

We use a simple acronym to encourage body acceptance: I AM OK.

I	*Indignation*
A	*Awareness*
M	*Maturity*
O	*Opportunity*
K	*Kindness*

INDIGNATION. Indignation is a wonderful form of anger that informs us that something unfair and intrusive is occurring. The root of the word is *dignity*. We reclaim our personal dignity when we learn to question demands and pressures from outside that are unreasonable and damaging. Many media representations of beauty are just that—unreasonable and damaging. We counsel clients to question the gaunt faces that peer out from magazine racks.

AWARENESS. Many clients who struggle with self-image have extremely negative self-talk. One client discovered that before she went on a food binge she told herself she was "ugly and fat" and no one would ever love her. The food became a comfort for the harsh words she said to herself.

If you struggle with body image, start writing down what you are saying to yourself during a typical day. Remember to watch for the language of the Stressful Seven to see if you are operating under any of these thinking errors. Share your discoveries with a trusted friend and ask him or her to gently remind you to speak positively to yourself. Activate your inner guide to notice cruel words and turn them into affirming, loving statements.

MATURITY. One sure sign of maturity is the ability to question the wisdom and accuracy of authority figures. When we notice teenage models who are meant to represent adult fashion and beauty, we need to question the accuracy of that image. We have learned to question our politicians when we find them to be untrustworthy. We must learn to question the many media representations and stories that come our way each day with the same dogged search for truth. Maturity develops when we trust our own authority in situations that demand fairness.

OPPORTUNITY. Every time we face a challenge, we face an opportunity to grow and expand. When we naively accept that things are the way they are supposed to be, we lose opportunities for growth. Some people who recover from eating disorders call their disorder a gift, without which they may have missed an opportunity to become more authentic. We find truth in the old saying "adversity builds character."

KINDNESS. Self-hatred often underlies poor self-image. Somewhere in our development we learned to be harsh critics of others and ourselves. It is up to each one of us to turn this harshness into loving-kindness. One way to create loving-kindness is to practice self-forgiveness. It is important to forgive ourselves for all the wrongs, real or imagined, we have committed. Research shows that some of the most successful individuals in the world attribute their success to a time of great personal failure. They believe this failure helped them on their path to success and happiness.

Part 4

TURNING DOWN THE HEAT ON TROUBLED RELATIONSHIPS

———

If your life works, you influence your family.
If your family works, your family influences
the community.
If your community works, your community
influences the nation.
If your nation works, your nation influences
the world.

John Heider

Dr. Dean Ornish dedicates his life to helping his patients reduce their chance of heart disease and heart attacks. He offers his clients prevention programs focused around diet, nutrition, and relaxation. Recently, Dr. Ornish stated that intimacy and connection with others is as great an indicator of good health as diet, exercise, or genetic predisposition. This is pretty powerful news. However, it isn't news to the many mental health professionals who witness the miracles wrought by intimacy and love in clients' recovery processes. ❈ Creating and maintaining a healthy network of relationships can literally be the difference between life and death. This is backed up by research into the custom of shunning or banishment. In the Amish communities, certain serious crimes are punishable by banishment. The accused is exiled from his or her friends, family, and community. Social researchers studied the lives of these exiles and discovered that their average life span, after they were exiled, was dramatically less than that of the members who remained in the community.

Chapter 16

The Essential Community

―――――

BETH'S STORY: *Alone on a Mountaintop*

Beth has a lifelong war with her weight; it is a war she is losing. She recently ended a four-year relationship with her partner who lived five hours away from her small mountain town on the Western Slope of Colorado. Beth gained forty pounds after the breakup and is at an all-time high of two hundred pounds. Her love of outdoor sports and travel and her overall health are seriously compromised by her weight. Her doctor advised her to lose weight and try an antidepressant. Beth has been on the antidepressant for two months and is beginning to feel more energetic. However, she is afraid she will slip back into her depression if she goes off the drug.

Beth has a plan; she wants to lose the weight, understand her depression, and then create a new community of friends. Like many people in her situation, she is attempting to put the cart before the horse. First, she needs to create a community. Her other goals will be much easier to achieve when she has the support of loving friends and family to help her.

Many people who seek counseling have incomplete community connections. They may be isolated or overwhelmed by relationships that leave them tired and empty or they may have few if any close connections. They are unaware how much this adds to feelings of loneliness, depression, anxiety, and frustration. In fact, many clients who abuse drugs, alcohol, and food often have insufficient community support. If you think avoiding relationships will keep your stress level down, think again.

We counsel clients to create a visual representation of community in order to chart the people currently inhabiting their world. The client draws a rainbow on the page, like the one below. The client occupies the center of the rainbow, and community members are arranged in ascending bands near or far according to the intimacy with the client.

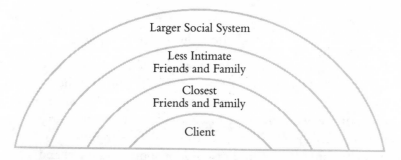

Larger Social System

Less Intimate
Friends and Family

Closest
Friends and Family

Client

Think back to Beth's story. She was attempting to lose weight and alleviate her depression prior to building a community. We encouraged her to look at her current community to evaluate her support system before she attempted to tackle these changes. In the band closest to the center, Beth placed the names of those people who are most intimate with her. These are the people who will be there for her in a crisis, no questions asked. They could be family members, friends, old classmates, and so on.

In the next band, Beth placed the names of people less intimate than those in the inner circle. These were probably not people she would ask for money or help or share her deepest secrets with. They would be less likely to jump in if Beth was having a crisis. Nevertheless, they occupy a place in Beth's social world. In the outer band, Beth listed the names of more distant acquaintances, perhaps people she sees only once in a great while or coworkers who are not necessarily close. This list includes people in her larger social circle whom she would not refer to as intimate or close.

Beth came to recognize her self-imposed isolation and worked diligently to assess and reevaluate her relationships. She began to understand how essential community support was for her healing process. She was encouraged by the information that she could make changes that would affect her mood, weight, social life, and spiritual practice. Isolation is a strong factor in most eating disorders, and the first step in Beth's healing was to examine her current community.

Beth's Community Rainbow

Beth noticed her closest band contained only biological family members: members who required a lot of her time and energy. The middle band was empty, and the outer band contained distant friends that she communicated with once or twice a year. She remarked that there seemed to be few people whom she could count on in a pinch and almost no one that she could call a good friend. Her isolation was suddenly palpable to her.

Next, Beth created a new set of rainbows to represent where she would like people to be a year from now. Some people may move further away from her; some may move closer. Others may leave the bands altogether, and new people may take their places. Then she made a list of new friends to add within the next twelve months. Her final step was to create an ideal community as a lifetime goal. Her new community was diverse, rich, and vibrant. Notice how her community changes with each rainbow.

Beth's One-Year Plan

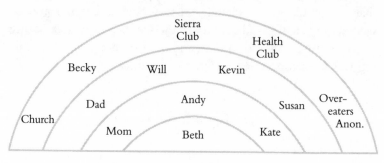

Beth's Ideal Community Rainbow

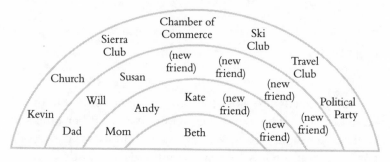

LEANN'S STORY: *The Compromised Caretaker*

Leann is a petite thirty-eight-year-old mother of three who works full-time in the children's ward of a Denver-area hospital as a registered nurse. She comes to therapy exhausted and anxious. In a session, I ask Leann to describe a typical day in her life. She reports that she spends most of her day attending to the needs of patients, her children, and an ailing father and doing endless chores. Leann is instructed to diagram the energy flow between her and the people and tasks in her community. This might help Leann understand why she is so exhausted.

It is not enough simply to have a community abundant with names. A key ingredient of a healthy community is the flow of energy from you to the other people in your rainbow and back again. Energy flow is simply the amount of support, love, and intimacy that flows from one person to another. In a well-balanced flow of energy, as much energy flows out as flows in.

When energy flow is well-balanced in your life, the energy that flows from you to other people is returned. It is important to keep in mind that energy flowing into your life does not have to come from the same people you are giving to. For example, young children take a great deal of your energy almost by design. One way to get energy back might be to get yourself a massage every month. There is not just one answer for everyone; the goal is to look at where your energy is going and where it is coming from. The bottom line is balancing energy flow. The next drawing will show you how to chart energy flow within your rainbow.

COMMUNITY ENERGY FLOW

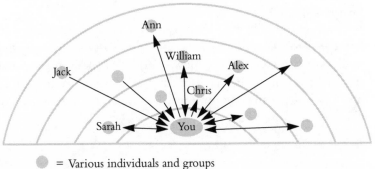

= Various individuals and groups
= Direction of energy flow
= Balanced energy flow

The relationships that take energy from you are represented by arrows pointing away from the band marked "YOU." This includes the relationships with Ann and Chris in the diagram. The relationships that give energy to you are represented by arrows pointing toward the band marked "YOU." This includes the relationship with Jack. If relationships are fairly balanced in terms of giving and receiving energy, the arrows point both ways. This is represented by the relationships with William, Alex, and Sarah.

Let's see how charting her energy flow helps Leann understand her exhaustion. Leann was instructed to fill in the energy flow on her rainbow. She drew the energy flow arrows and stepped back to look. To her amazement, there was not one arrow pointing toward her. The visual representation of her life brought sobs of frustration and resentment. Suddenly, she could see the way her community was draining her. Armed with this awareness, she could begin to bring more balance to her community.

Over a series of months, Leann successfully eliminated the most draining relationships and created more give and take in others. Most important, she was able to bring in relationships in which others gave more to her than they took. For instance, she treated herself to a massage once a week, joined a women's yoga class, and brought her husband into counseling to help teach both of them how to give more when either one was feeling depleted.

Leann felt empowered by her success in creating balance in her life. She found the energy and time to pursue her secret passion of jazz dancing. Her new energy flow demonstrates her success at changing her relationships and invariably her entire life. Look at Leann's community rainbows to note how she changes the flow of energy.

Leann's Current Energy Flow

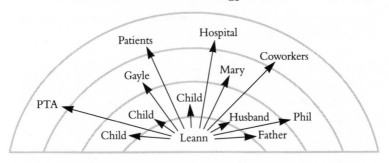

Leann's New Energy Flow

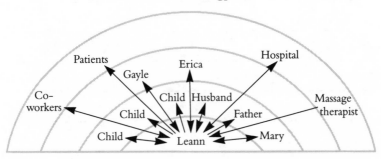

WHO IS IN *YOUR* LIFE?

Let's imagine you just received news that your father is ill and you must fly home tonight. Whom will you call? Who will take care of the house while you are gone? Who will take you to the airport? Who will listen while you talk through your fears? Is there anyone who will loan you money to fly home? We hope you have more than a few good friends who would step in. We all need community connections to live a stress-free life. You've seen how Beth and Leann did it. Now it's your turn. The following exercises will lead you through the creation of a community of *your* choosing.

On page 136, you will find three columns in which to list names. List the names of all your friends, family members, acquaintances, affiliations, and groups according to how close they are to you. Column 1 includes people or groups closest to you, Column 3 includes those more distant, and Column 2 is somewhere in between.

Column 1   *Column 2*   *Column 3*

_____   _____   _____

_____   _____   _____

_____   _____   _____

_____   _____   _____

_____   _____   _____

_____   _____   _____

_____   _____   _____

_____   _____   _____

_____   _____   _____

BUILD YOUR IDEAL COMMUNITY

Now you have the names to help you build your community rainbow. This rainbow will show you where your family and friends are placed in terms of intimacy. In the set of rainbows on page 137, place the people in Column 1 in the band closest to you. In the next band, place Column 2 people. In the outer band, place Column 3 people. This gives you a picture of what your community looks like in the present moment.

Your Current Community Rainbow

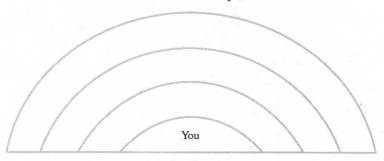

Now return to this rainbow and add arrows to show the flow of energy between you and the people in your community. Remember that arrows pointing away from you indicate you are mostly giving energy, arrows pointing toward you mean the other person is mostly giving energy to you, and arrows pointing to both you and the other person indicate a balanced flow of energy. If you notice an imbalance in one band or another, you may want to add or take away some people. Take a moment to look at the picture of your community. Does it seem balanced? Are there too few or too many people in one or more bands? Is the energy flow pretty well-balanced? If it is unbalanced, is that okay with you? If not, the next exercise will help you create a more vibrant community.

Use the community rainbow on page 138 to create the community you wish to have in the next twelve months. Maybe you want to add one person to your inner circle. Maybe you want to move someone in the inner band out or someone from the outer band in. Perhaps you want to join a club to bring into your community section. Maybe you want to resign from a group you've been involved with. Take a moment to fill in this one-year goal of your community.

Your One-Year Community Goal

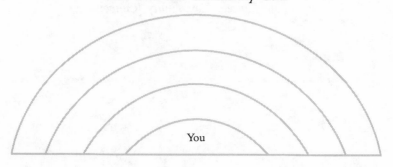

You

In this final rainbow you get to create an ideal community. Think big! Include whomever you want, even if it seems impossible. Take a moment to let yourself dream of your ideal community. Let this be a reminder of all you want in a community and all you deserve!

Your Ideal Community Rainbow

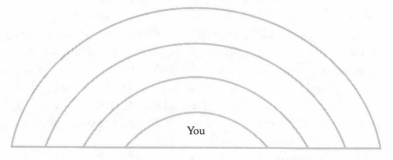

You

Chapter 17

Healthy Communities Equal Healthy Boundaries

—

BILL'S STORY: *The Confused Widower*

Bill looks like he hasn't slept in days. Two weeks ago his daughter ran away from home and his son was caught shoplifting at a grocery store. Bill's wife died two years ago in a car accident, and he has tried to manage the family since her death. He began to withdraw after his wife's death, particularly from his daughter. Bill has no idea how to raise his daughter, so he sets strict limits for her and lets the boys run wild. Not surprisingly, the family pot boiled over. Tempers flared, emotional outbursts grew frequent, and Bill's daughter felt abandoned and angry.

Bill did not understand how crucial personal boundaries are to healthy relationships. For instance, what would happen if a stranger suddenly jumped over your privacy fence and started toward your house? You might be startled, frightened, angry, or confused. You might shout at him, "What do you think you're doing in my yard?!" You know he has stepped over your boundary.

Boundaries can also be abstract lines that separate one person from another. These types of boundaries are difficult for some people to comprehend because they cannot see or touch them. However, most of us can feel when an abstract boundary has been crossed or violated.

Abstract boundaries might be physical, emotional, or verbal. Boundaries may be referred to as "personal space" or "limits." Regardless of the terminology, they are essential to healthy, supportive relationships.

Boundaries protect your physical, emotional, and mental well-being in the same way that your fence protects your home. But many of us never learn to set clear, direct boundaries. Bill's case demonstrates the necessity of boundaries, especially with children!

In his initial session, the core of Bill's trouble with parenthood emerged as an inability to negotiate limits for his children. Bill learned about boundaries and how a parent sets them with children. He began to practice setting limits with the boys at family counseling sessions. He also learned how to listen to his daughter without becoming angry. He practiced letting her have more privileges and confessed that "all this emotional stuff used to be handled by my wife." As Bill set new boundaries, his relationships with his kids grew more intimate and more rewarding. He actually started to enjoy being a parent. He also learned how to avoid the following common violations.

FOUR COMMON BOUNDARY VIOLATIONS

Boundary violations can take many forms. Some of the more obvious forms of boundary violations are physical assaults, unsolicited touch, verbal abuse, and stealing. However, it is the subtler forms that make up most of the daily boundary violations we all encounter. Clients often remark that nothing is worse than the feeling of becoming lost (losing the boundaries between themselves and the other person) in a relationship. There is a solution. It begins with recognizing and setting clear, consistent boundaries, both internally and externally. Anyone can learn to set good boundaries. It takes a little know-how and practice. This process begins with awareness of the different kinds of boundary violations that work against us.

During a couple's session, one partner complained that she was infuriated when she arrived home from a hard day of work to a messy house, no signs of dinner, and her partner and kids slumped in front of the television. Her strategy was to storm upstairs, throw on her sweats, and furiously clean the house and prepare supper. During dinner she began to cry uncontrollably. She was at the end of her rope.

Her children and husband were confused. They had no idea she wanted them to pitch in more. She never asked for help, and when it did not arrive she felt violated and betrayed. This represents the first common boundary violation: *making the deadly assumption.*

A second form of boundary violation is called *too much, too soon.* This happens when someone makes a communication error of eliciting or providing too much information, far too soon. Some people report a feeling of nausea when other people either ask too many personal questions or spill their life stories in the first few moments of meeting.

A third form of boundary violation is *the giveaway.* This occurs when people employ passive communication and say yes to a request for a favor when inside they are screaming no. It is important to remember that the person who asks the favor is not the villain. The person who gives the false yes is victimizing him- or herself. Personal integrity means owning responsibility and correcting this boundary violation.

A final subtle violation of boundaries is called *gossip.* Virginia Satir, the late, internationally acclaimed family therapist, remarked at a conference, "Gossip is evil." Satir believed nothing good ever came of gossip and that families should be told the same. Gossip is a violation of the person being talked about and a violation of the relationship between the two people who are gossiping. Again, clients have reported feelings of nausea after listening to or participating in the verbal ambush of a friend or coworker behind his or her back. Personal integrity is about honest communication, not creating a conspiracy be-hind the scenes.

Boundaries are ultimately about intimacy, because without healthy boundaries true intimacy cannot occur. You cannot trust someone who trounces on your personal space, nor can you trust yourself to stay safe if you do not prevent others from violating your boundaries. Some of us have trouble asking for help and making close friends because we never learned to es-tablish clear boundaries between others and ourselves. Others let people in too close or too quickly and then feel violated. Some of us dive into a relationship, not realizing it may be like a driving surf that leaves us stripped and vulnerable and uncer-emoniously deposited on a hard beach.

HOW TO RECOGNIZE BOUNDARY VIOLATIONS

Read the list below and circle the boundary errors you are most likely to make. This will make you more aware the next time you cross one of these boundaries.

1. "Telling all" or talking at an intimate level on first meeting someone.
2. "Falling in love" with a new acquaintance or anyone who reaches out.
3. Being overwhelmed by a person, preoccupied with thoughts of him or her.
4. Acting on first sexual impulse or having sex with someone when you do not want to. You are doing it simply to please the other person.
5. Going against personal values or rights to please others.
6. Not noticing when someone else invades your boundaries.
7. Taking as much as you can get for the sake of getting, or allowing others to take as much as they can from you.
8. Touching a person or letting him or her touch you with-out asking.

9. Letting others direct your life, describe your reality, or define you.
10. Believing others can anticipate your needs or fill them automatically.
11. Feeling depressed or guilty when you say no.
12. Allowing someone to put you down or to shame you.
13. Not speaking up when you feel uncomfortable or abused.
14. Feeling responsible for the behaviors of another.
15. Abusing your body with food, sex, alcohol, or drugs.

STRENGTHENING BOUNDARIES

Take a moment to take this test of your boundaries. Check the items that describe you. You can tell when you are beginning to strengthen your boundaries when you check any of the following:

____ You are comfortable receiving from others as well as giving.

____ You act on your feelings when you need to.

____ You don't take things personally. If a partner has a wandering eye or a friend is rude to you, you understand this action has more to do with the other person than with you.

____ You can say no when you want without feeling a great amount of guilt.

____ You do not blame yourself for everything that goes wrong in a relationship or friendship.

____ You generally do what you want to do rather than depending on the suggestions or demands of others.

____ You no longer feel responsible for making a relationship work or making the other person happy.

____ You might disagree with a friend or colleague and still maintain a healthy relationship with him or her.

____ You realize that you are not responsible for the actions of other people.

Setting healthy boundaries is a direction. It takes time to recognize where and when you have passive or rigid boundaries. It also takes practice to set healthy, flexible boundaries. Remember, each time you set a healthy boundary you increase your self-esteem and confidence and decrease your stress! The next chapter describes a form of boundary violation that is more important to recognize and defuse than any other: the triangle.

Chapter 18

Triangles

ALICE'S STORY: *People Make Me Crazy*

One night, Alice aimed her speeding car at a bridge embankment. Paramedics were amazed to see her emerge uninjured from the tangled metal. They were not surprised to smell the alcohol on her breath, and she was booked quickly for a DUI. Alice came to therapy as part of her court sentence. She appeared almost cheerful at her interview, acting as if her attempted suicide was a small misstep. "It was a little thing," she tried to assure her caseworker.

A couple of weeks into therapy, Alice exclaimed, "People make me crazy!" She felt her relationships were out of control and suicide was the only remaining option. Alice felt trapped at home with her husband and their little girl; both of whom treated Alice like a slave. Her other children—two sons—were living with their father and had little regard for or awareness of Alice's needs. Alice's ex-husband demanded that she spend every moment of her visitation days driving the kids all around town. Alice hated her work and often found herself trapped between two coworkers or a coworker and her boss.

There is one form of boundary violation that is more important to recognize and defuse than any other: the triangle. According to Lawrence Shulman, author of *The Skills of Helping*, triangulation is "a process in which one party attempts to gain the allegiance of a second party, in the struggle with a third party . . ." Let's take a closer look at this issue. How do people communicate when they are afraid to be assertive? Usually they find a third person to carry the message. This creates triangulation. Soon triangles become entrenched, and the three people involved lose intimacy with one another.

In certain triangles, one person assumes the role of the victim, another the villain, and the third the rescuer. Police have long understood the importance of recognizing the danger of this kind of triangle. More police are hurt or killed in domestic violence calls than in any other duty, because the fighting lovers or friends draw police into a type of fluid triangulation. The rescuing police officer knows very well that he or she may suddenly become the villain during a domestic violence call.

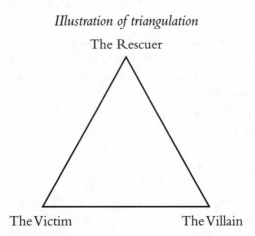

Illustration of triangulation

The Rescuer

The Victim   The Villain

This happens when the abused individual watches the police try to subdue the villain, who happens to be the victim's lover or spouse. Suddenly the officer looks like a villain and the villain looks like a helpless victim. The wife switches from victim to rescuer and may pick up a gun or knife and attack the officer. After all, it is the villainous partner who is now the victim in need of rescue. Police have learned from this tragic experience to neutralize the triangle by quickly separating the warring couple.

Triangulation begins at birth when we are positioned between mom and dad. Many clients report that the triangle that began at birth hardens into set roles for parents and child that are next to impossible to change. Many of us carry this tendency to triangulate into adult relationships. In Alice's case this triangulation almost led to her taking her own life.

Alice needed to find a few areas of control in her life. These areas were the many triangles she felt trapped in at home, at work, and with her kids. Alice was instructed to draw every triangle she was involved in on the chalkboard. Then she named her role in every triangle: victim, villain, or rescuer. After about fifteen minutes, the chalkboard was packed with triangles. Not one relationship was free of some kind of triangle. Alice was shocked and overwhelmed.

She had taken her first step out of the trap her life had become. Just as she had helped to create every triangle, she could disassemble them, one by one. The next step was to find out when this pattern of triangulation began. Alice explained that the pattern started with her parents many years ago. Her father was very strict and was often in conflict with Alice. Her mother came to Alice's defense and demanded her husband lighten up on their daughter. Alice often felt like a tennis ball flying from side to side in her parents' verbal battles. Triangles had become a bad habit, but one Alice felt she could give up.

It was time to disassemble these triangles. She began with her husband. Alice had the unpleasant role of the villain, because she was the disciplinarian in the family. Alice's daughter was angry with her, especially when daddy came in to rescue his "little girl" from her. Alice agreed to stop disciplining the girl and wait until her husband was at his wit's end. Chances were good that he would step in and do the disciplining. Eventually, he did get the message and began to take more leader-ship in raising their daughter.

Next, Alice tackled her sons and her ex-husband. Alice told her sons that she was not available until after 2 P.M. on her days off. She told her ex-husband he was no longer to tell her how to parent and that pitting the boys against her would result in a court battle. Over the course of several months, Alice learned to step out of triangles, set healthy boundaries, and take much-needed time for herself. Not surprisingly, her suicidal thoughts diminished and she began to enjoy her work and home life.

CHART YOUR TRIANGLES

Now it's your turn to explore unhealthy triangles. On page 149 you will find four blank triangles. Fill in the names of the four most troublesome triangles you find yourself in. Match the role (rescuer, victim, and villain) to each name. If you join with someone and gossip about another person, it's a good in-dication that there is a triangle.

HOW TO STEP OUT OF TRIANGLES

The method for stopping your involvement in triangles is sim-ple. When someone approaches you because he or she is angry at someone else, ask yourself three questions:

1. Do I want to become the rescuer in this situation?
2. Will this adversely affect my relationship with either per-son involved?
3. Is this someone I often get into triangles with?

Then ask the person if you can share the information with the person you are talking about. The next step is simply to say you are not comfortable hearing about this argument. If you can, take this opportunity to explain about triangles and why you do not want to participate. Assure the person that

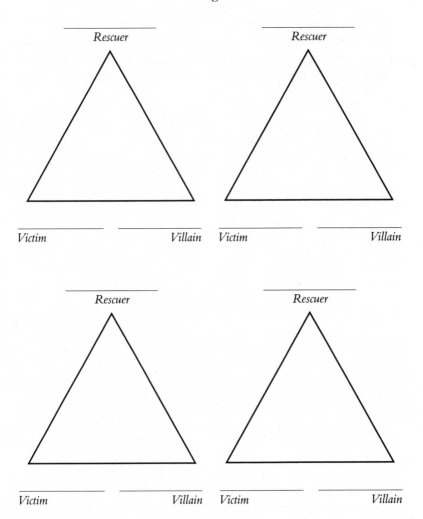

you are supportive of his situation but are staying out of the triangle to help yourself. Lead by example and he will understand.

Boundaries are essential to a healthy community, yet many of us struggle with how to set them. A great deal of the problem stems from our inability to be assertive with people in our lives. Clear, assertive communication is the only way to set a boundary and make it stick while keeping the relationship with the other person intact. In the next chapter, you will learn the basics of assertiveness.

Chapter 19

Assertiveness: The Key to Building Community

MARIA'S STORY: *The Silent Volcano*

Maria describes herself as a silent volcano. She came to therapy after receiving many criticisms of her communication skills from family, friends, and coworkers. She feels hurt and confused by the criticism and wants to understand what she is doing wrong. She is asked to describe how she responds to another person's anger. "Well," she muses, "I would be hurt and probably withdraw until they calmed down. Later, I'd let them have it with both barrels!"

Maria is describing a typical passive-aggressive response to conflict. She responds first by withdrawing and most likely letting her hurt and anger build for a while. When the anger becomes intolerable, she explodes and attacks the person with "both barrels." It is difficult to maintain healthy relationships with this type of response pattern.

You have probably heard of seminars offered by business organizations on the subject of assertiveness training. There is a good reason these seminars continue to be popular. Nonassertive communication leads to most of the stress experienced in interpersonal relationships. Think about that for a minute. Just by learning how to talk and behave more assertively, you will reduce most of the stress you experience in your relationships! We think that's a pretty good motivator for change.

Many of us fall into the trap of not speaking our mind or stating our needs in certain situations and ending up angry at ourselves and resentful toward others. Assertiveness means asking for what you need, when you need it. It's that simple. It does not mean demanding what you want—that's aggression. And it does not mean being so nice that the other person doesn't take you seriously—that is being passive.

Say you are watching a movie at the theater and some people behind you keep talking. Nonassertive behavior is to sit quietly, fume and mutter, and not enjoy the movie. An aggressive response would be to turn around and scream, "Shut up, you idiots!" The result would be alienation and maybe a fight. Assertiveness would be a simple, firm statement like "please stop talking during the movie."

INEFFECTIVE COMMUNICATION

Take a moment to read through the following list of ineffective communication methods. Notice if you talk to others in any of these ways. Circle the ones that apply.

1. *Passive aggression.* You save up your hurts and complaints and then explode at the person or get back at her indirectly.
2. *Blame.* You are sure it is the other person's fault and tell him so.
3. *Fixing.* Instead of listening to the other person, you respond with advice and try to help or "fix" her.
4. *Name calling.* You use demeaning words during an argument meant to diminish the other person, such as *idiot, fool,* or *loser.*
5. *Denial.* You claim you don't feel a certain way when, in fact, you do.

6. *Defeat.* You give up and withdraw during discussions.
7. *Sarcasm.* You use a biting sense of humor to make your point, usually at another person's expense.
8. *Kitchen-sinking.* You divert the conversation into a list of past hurts and trespasses that have little to do with the here and now.
9. *Superiority.* You suggest the other person has the problem and refuse to admit to any wrongdoing on your part.
10. *Self-blame.* You act as if you are a terrible person to avoid dealing with the problem at hand.
11. *Globalizing.* You make all-or-nothing statements that render the situation hopeless, for example, *"This always happens; you always say that."*
12. *Assuming.* You expect the other person to know what you want, expect, or mean, even though you do not directly let your needs be known.

Now that you know what *not* to do, here are some guidelines for changing your behavior from ineffective aggression or passivity to life-changing assertiveness.

HOW TO BEHAVE ASSERTIVELY

1. Make sure your no means no. Don't let people guess whether you mean it or not. You might explain why it is a no, but don't be unduly apologetic.
2. Be brief and concise when replying to questions or concerns.
3. Insist on equal and fair treatment.
4. Use proper body assertiveness. For example, make eye contact with the person you are addressing. Check your other body language for behavior that might convey indirectness or lack of self-assurance (e.g., hand over mouth, shuffling feet). Watch your tone of voice and inflection, making sure you speak in neither an inaudible whisper nor an overly loud voice.

5. If a request seems unfair, ask for an explanation.
6. Separate the person from the behavior when you express annoyance or criticism. The behavior is what you don't like, not the person.
7. Try to use "I statements" when commenting on someone else's behavior. For instance, you might say, "*I feel hurt when you miss appointments because it seems like you don't care.*"
8. Keep a journal of your progress and follow these key points:
   A. Write down what works.
   B. Find good role models to observe.
   C. Practice with safe people.
   D. Be curious, not judgmental, about your mistakes.
   E. Reward yourself for working on assertiveness, no matter what the results.
9. Be congruent. If you feel a certain way inside, express it outside (if appropriate). If you don't think your behavior is appropriate, check it out with a few people to make sure you are not merely being passive.

BODY-MIND ASSERTIVENESS

JOEL'S STORY: *That Ole Hangdog Look*

Joel was a timid, nervous student at the University of Colorado, studying research medicine. He came to therapy because of great difficulties with personal relationships. The main issue was that he felt people did not hear him or take him seriously. He felt ignored and abused by other classmates. One day I was driving down Pearl Street and noticed Joel on the sidewalk. His posture could best be described as an "ole hangdog look." His eyes were pointed down to his slowly shuffling feet, his head hanging forward and shoulders slumped.

The next session, I reported to Joel what I noticed and demonstrated his posture for him. Then I had him stand up and recreate the hangdog look. Slowly, I instructed him to move into a more assertive posture: shoulders back, head level, eyes looking straight at me. Then he played with moving in and out of these two postures. He began to chuckle softly. "Jeez, I feel like a bug on the bottom of someone's shoe when I stand all slumped over. But when I stand up straight . . . I feel like a man."

What does your body language communicate to others? What do you notice about the way others use their bodies to communicate? You communicate a great deal of information by the way you stand and move your body, by the ways you contort your face, and through your eye contact or lack thereof. Interviews with criminals who snatch purses or mug individuals reveal a fascinating fact. These criminals say they can tell by the way people stand and hold themselves whether or not they will be easy victims or fighters. A potential victim with an assertive posture is one they will avoid every time. We have a quick and easy program for you we call Body-Mind Assertiveness.

The Assertive Posture

The best posture for assertiveness is a relaxed and balanced stance in which the body neither fidgets nor freezes in place. Here are five simple steps for a relaxed and assertive posture:

1. Breathe steadily.
2. Pull your shoulders back and down by lowering your shoulder blades.
3. Keep your head level.
4. Keep your knees bent and relaxed.
5. Stand with your feet shoulder-width apart.

The Assertive Face

A relaxed face with a level chin is the best way to communicate assertiveness. Here are some simple steps for a relaxed, assertive face:

1. Keep your chin level.
2. Watch out for excessive swallowing or lip wetting.
3. Watch for excessive throat clearing or tensing of facial muscles. (These can give the signal that you are nervous or ill at ease.)
4. Try this facial relaxation: Soften your eyes by slightly raising your eyebrows and then relaxing them. Keep your gaze soft and relaxed. Keep your chin level.

Practice this at home along with your assertive posture.

The Assertive Gaze

Make eye contact with the person you are communicating with. Your eyes should be soft and direct. No staring contests! Remember, a soft and direct gaze communicates confidence and courage. Practice this with a friend. If you find it difficult, don't worry. Eye contact takes time and practice. Soon it will feel as natural as breathing!

We want to end the assertiveness piece by stating your Assertiveness Bill of Rights. We suggest you copy this list and put it on your refrigerator or mirror. If you remember these rights, you are halfway to being a fully assertive human being.

The Assertiveness Bill of Rights

The most difficult thing about assertiveness is not learning *how* to be assertive, but learning *when* to be assertive. The following list offers some ideals in terms of assertiveness; however, it is important to keep in mind that good judgment is necessary in all situations. If you want to practice being assertive, pick your battles carefully!

1. The right to put yourself first.
2. The right to select your own lifestyle.
3. The right to make mistakes.
4. The right to decide whether your feelings are right for you.

5. The right to hold your own opinions and beliefs.
6. The right to change your mind and do things differently.
7. The right to protest unfair treatment.
8. The right to interrupt and ask questions.
9. The right to ask for help.
10. The right to feel and express your distress.
11. The right to ignore what others tell you.
12. The right to receive credit for a job well done.
13. The right to say no and not meet the needs of others.
14. The right to be alone when you want to be.
15. The right not to have to justify yourself to others.
16. The right not to get involved in others' concerns.
17. The right not to be overly sensitive to others' needs.
18. The right not to care what other people think about you.
19. The right to choose not to answer someone.
20. THE RIGHT TO BE ASSERTIVE.

A strong, supportive, and vibrant community is essential to a stress-free lifestyle. It is not a matter of simply making new friends. It involves a commitment to set healthy boundaries, step out of destructive triangles, and balance the energy flow within your community. Setting boundaries is not only helpful in keeping out physical danger and violation; it is important for preventing the more subtle violations of *making the deadly assumption; the giveaway; too much, too soon;* and *gossip.*

You have everything you need to build a healthy community. What you must do is take responsibility for knowing your own limits and then get feedback from others. You can have a community based on personal integrity in which what you think becomes what you feel, becomes what you say, becomes how you behave. In this way, friends and family will seldom have to guess your motives and will know just where your limits are. In the end, your integrity is the foundation on which your life will be built.

Chapter 20

Partnership

How Did We Get Here?

Kelly and Brad arrived for their first session and sat on opposite ends of the couch. When asked what brought them to therapy, Kelly replied, "We just can't communicate anymore!" Brad nodded his head in silent agreement. Brad was asked how they met. He reported that they met while working on the campaign staff of a local congressman. He admitted thinking Kelly was "drop-dead gorgeous" when he first met her. "I loved how much we thought alike and shared the same dreams and values," he marveled. Kelly was asked what attracted her to Brad. "Oh," she said, "his search for truth, his honesty and integrity. And of course, he has those beautiful blue eyes." They both smiled and softened.

When asked what they hoped to get from therapy, they each expressed a desire to learn to communicate better. It seems that their conversations had slowly gone from loving wonder to critical evaluations and bringing up past hurts to each other. Like most breakdowns in couples' communication, it happened one degree at a time. Kelly and Brad had some difficult but rewarding work ahead of them. Their intervention was to go home and make separate lists of all the big and little hurts they felt the other caused them and then bring these back to therapy. In order for them to stay together, they needed to find mutual forgiveness. It was time to bury the hurts and end the ineffective communication style of "kitchen-sinking": bringing up past hurts in the middle of an argument about something that is happening in the present.

It is difficult to create movement in a couples' session when either person is holding onto past injustices. One or both of them end up living in a past that cannot be changed. This makes dealing with the present a daunting task. When Brad and Kelly returned to therapy, they shared their lists of past hurts with each another. They then created a practice of letting go: They burned the sheets of paper, containing their hurts, in their fireplace and pledged to let go of all the wrongs the other had committed. Each began to cry as the paper burned. They asked for and granted each other forgiveness. Brad and Kelly had accomplished this important first step and were ready to deal with the present issues and concerns of their couplehood.

TOGETHERNESS AND SEPARATENESS

Clients in couples counseling often swing between opposite fears: the fear of abandonment and the fear of engulfment. Sometimes they express both fears in a single session, fears that seem to contradict one another. These fears are quite understandable when we take them for what they are, primal fears from infancy. Abandonment in infancy is death; engulfment in infancy means loss of self. These are frightening fears that we often apply to our adult relationships. The link between our childhood experiences and our adult fears may be forgotten on a conscious level and unknowingly acted out with our partners.

These two fears are often the basis of intimacy issues in relationships. Many couples become paralyzed if they perceive that the only choices in a relationship are to be abandoned or to be engulfed by the other. Sometimes the expectant fear becomes so overwhelming that one person initiates a behavior that creates abandonment or engulfment. What a couple misses in these moments of terror are the many opportunities to face their fears and grow, both as a couple and as individuals.

DIFFERENTIATION: A SOLUTION TO TOGETHERNESS AND SEPARATENESS

When couples swing back and forth between fear of abandonment and fear of engulfment, they miss out on a major benefit of relationships: differentiation. Differentiation is the process whereby a couple rediscovers individual needs and traits that were lost within the relationship. Many of us operate under the myth that when we join in intimate relationships we must lose our individual identity. Nothing could be further from the truth. A relationship may be one of the few settings in which we can truly discover our individuality.

When we are alone, we assume we know who we are and what we are made of. Then we form a relationship and find ourselves behaving in ways we never imagined we would. How does this happen? One degree at a time. Certain fears surface only in relationships and can simmer for years until we notice the rising heat.

It's easy to lose yourself in a relationship. It is easy to put someone else first at the expense of your own needs. It is just as easy to maintain a separateness that precludes real intimacy, especially when you do not tell the other person what is on your mind and in your heart. Success is achieved when both intimacy and selfhood are maintained in relationships with others. Differentiation is a process, not a goal. It may take the entire life of your relationship to find out who you are, alone and together. The good news is that people who undertake this process can have the most exciting and rewarding relationships of all.

IMBALANCE OF POWER IN MONEY AND SEX

There is one area of a relationship in which complete equity must be achieved—the sharing of power. Healthy relationships are based on sharing power in various aspects of daily life. Like it or not, in this society there is a growing distinction between economic classes, which are defined by money, education, and social power.

One of the most common power imbalances we have found in relationships is that of different income levels. Financial imbalance in a relationship can tear at a couple's trust, personal power, and sense of togetherness. The income disparity may be due to differences in educational levels, giving one person an intellectual and economic advantage over the other. Often the person who makes less money will feel a loss of power and influence in the relationship. Many couples who come to therapy have never considered how this affects their feelings for one another.

In couples counseling, we encourage individuals to evaluate where the power is held in terms of earning potential, control of finances, social decision making, sex, child rearing, and other major aspects of the relationship. Couples need to find a way to balance the distribution of power within their relationship or the union will begin to collapse under the inequity.

How to Equalize the Power in Income Levels

Resentment can build quickly if both people are contributing equally to household expenses when there is a sizable difference in take-home pay. A host of problems can be avoided if the issue of income disparity is addressed from the start of the relationship.

Kelly and Brad never considered the impact of the sizable difference in their salaries. Brad, a junior partner in a law firm, earned $75,000 annually. Kelly, on the other hand, earned $25,000 annually at her job as a grade school teacher.

They each derived great pleasure and satisfaction from their respective careers and realized there would always be a discrepancy in income. They contributed equally to the monthly bills, which were fairly modest at first. However, as Brad began to make more money, they moved to a more expensive home, purchased a new car, and traveled more often, but they made no adjustment in terms of their monthly contribution.

After taxes and retirement deductions, Kelly brought home $1,500 and Brad brought home $4,500. This meant that their total monthly income as a couple was $6,000. They had a good budget in place, which came to about $4,000 each month. If they both contributed 50 percent to the bills, Brad had $2,500 at the end of the month and Kelly was $500 short! After a time, Kelly watched her debt grow with the increasing monthly budget. She began to ask Brad for money for extras like haircuts, clothing, and lunches with friends.

Brad did not notice the increase in bills because he still kept a big chunk of his money at the end of each month. Kelly complained that she felt asking Brad for a share of his money reminded her of asking her dad for an allowance. Brad was oblivious to her distress because he felt his money was her money. They were able to solve the growing rift by following these simple steps:

1. Kelly and Brad figured out what percentage of the total income they each contributed monthly. Brad earned 75 percent and Kelly 25 percent of the total amount. In order for the budget to be equitable, they were counseled to use this percentage to divide the monthly bills. Kelly would contribute 25 percent to each bill, and Brad 75 percent.

2. Twice each month, on the 15th and 30th, Kelly and Brad had a "budget breakfast" at home. They would sit down with the monthly bills and each write checks from their respective accounts.

At the end of the month, Kelly had $500 left, removing the need to ask Brad for financial help. Brad still had $1500 left and was willing to contribute an additional thousand to a family savings fund for vacations, splurges, or emergencies.

You Can Create Financial Equity

Brad and Kelly's solution represents one way couples might create financial equity within their relationship. The following steps are suggestions. You must determine together which, if any, of these will work in your relationship:

1. Determine your combined monthly earnings.
2. Determine each person's percentage of the total earnings.
3. Determine your monthly budget (see Part 1, Chapter 4 for instructions on creating a monthly budget).
4. Establish two meetings a month to pay the bills together. (This keeps you both aware of where your money is going.)
5. Pay your percentage of each bill from your separate checking account. (We recommend separate accounts as a way of maintaining independence. After all, you don't want to have to explain a checkbook entry that is actually a surprise gift.)
6. Decide as a couple what you want to do with the money left over. If you are earning significantly more than your partner, consider contributing more to a joint family venture.

Sex

The bedroom can easily become the battleground for small and large imbalances that make up a relationship. If you are able to settle your financial differences and issues of raising children, you have a better chance of avoiding imbalances in your sexual relationship. If you don't pay attention to differences in power and influence, one or both partners may try to balance these out through sex. This may occur by withholding touch and sex from one another.

When the heat in the relationship rises in negative ways, the heat of passion often plummets. Stress can seriously inhibit sexual desire, as can stored resentment, body image issues, and negative thinking. These areas all tie together when we begin to share our physical selves with one another. If we are in balance emotionally, the sexual relationship will have a better chance of being in balance.

Steps to Take the Battle Out of the Bedroom

1. If you are storing old resentments, perform the ritual of writing them down, sharing them, and burning them once and for all like the couple at the beginning of this chapter.

2. Step out of the guilt and resentment game—in which one partner feels guilty for not wanting sexual contact as much as the other and the other partner feels resentment for not having his or her needs met. It takes two people to make or break sexual intimacy. Only when you both admit to needing change will there be progress.

3. Remember what attracted you to one another in the beginning of your relationship. How did you act toward each other then? What did you stop doing? What did you start doing?

4. Think of something in the area of touch and sexual connection that you used to enjoy but no longer engage in. Make a commitment to reintroduce this in your relationship.

5. Get away from the notion of orgasm as a measure of sexual success. The sexual relationship is far more encompassing and exciting than an orgasm.

6. Practice looking into each other's eyes when you make love.

7. Tell each other what you like sexually and what you don't like. Do not assume your partner can read your mind.

8. Try not to push away anxieties or fears. Talk about them, and slowly push your envelope of comfort.

9. Try just kissing one night. No matter how heated it gets, do not go any further. The idea is to reintroduce some anticipation and expectation into your relationship.

10. Try different things: ways of touching, new places, new positions, new music, oils, massages. Be creative as you celebrate one of our most joyous expressions of love and intimacy.

STEVE AND JILL'S STORY: *He Said, She Said*

Jill and Steve were a bright, articulate couple who were having trouble with their second child, Seth. Initially, they had taken Seth to a child psychologist. This counselor referred the parents for counseling to our offices. Jill and Steve were well matched and shared many of the same values and goals in life. They assumed these values would extend into child rearing. However, it became apparent that Jill had very different ideas from Steve about what was "good parenting."

Jill had had very strict parents who stifled a lot of her creativity as a child. She had made a secret pledge to allow her kids much more freedom. Steve was from the old school of tough love. He set demands on his children and expected them to follow through with little or no trouble. This marked difference in their values translated into Jill's caving in to the kids' wishes and Steve's angrily trying to impose order within the family. It was little wonder that Seth, at the impulsive age of thirteen, was "acting out." In fact, he was simply following the system that Jill and Steve had set up. He began to rebel against Steve's authority and pull Jill into a battle against Steve. He knew that his needs had a better chance of being met if he could convince Mom that Dad was a tyrant. This did not take much effort. Not surprisingly, Seth began to gain more and more power within the family and became increasingly defiant.

CHILD REARING

Steve and Jill had made a classic assumption early in their marriage—that they naturally would agree on the rules and limits involved in raising a family. This sets up a triangle for the child, who quickly learns that Mom and Dad do not agree on how to parent. When Seth became a teenager, the triangle was entrenched, and like a normal adolescent, he began to test the weak spots in the marriage and gain power in the family.

The introduction of children into a relationship often creates some measure of stress. The degree to which this new addition affects the relationship can be mitigated by an early agreement on how to rear the children. Each of us has had unique experiences when being raised by our own parents. Sifting through the best of those experiences and then combining those with our spouse's can be quite a task. Taking on this task can result in happier, healthier children.

When parents don't decide together how to raise their children, a triangle can easily develop. This triangle has the strict parent as the villain, the other parent as the rescuer, and the child as the victim. This type of triangle creates an imbalance in the family that the child can quickly turn to his or her advantage. If one parent is strict and the other lax, the child might learn to play them against each other to get what he or she wants.

This type of manipulation becomes a habit and will create havoc in the child's adult life. The child learns to communicate through manipulation and triangles. In the illustration following, the strict parent issues a demand to the child, who asks the other parent to reverse this demand. The parents then begin to argue over the demand. One solution to this problem is for the parents to agree not to reverse each other's decisions.

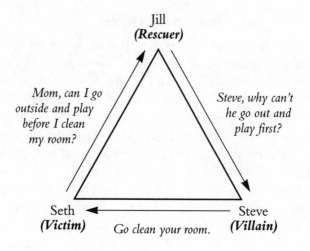

Jill
(Rescuer)

Mom, can I go outside and play before I clean my room?

Steve, why can't he go out and play first?

Seth
(Victim)

Go clean your room.

Steve
(Villain)

Notice how Seth uses his mother to try to get his way, circumventing his father's demands. This triangle weakens both the father's and the mother's authority, because the child learns that any demand can be overturned if he splits Mom and Dad. Over time, Jill and Steve were able to sit down and discuss ways to avoid this triangle. They each put their theories of child rearing on the table and discussed appropriate compromises.

Agreement on Raising the Children

1. Do not assume you know how your partner will parent the children. Discuss this issue before you decide to marry.

2. Create an open discussion of your experiences as a child. How were your parents successful? Where did they make mistakes? Decide what you liked the best and borrow their successes.

3. Never try to "make up" for your own childhood with your children. If you want to be different from your parents, that is fine, as long as it is not a reaction instead of a choice. Jill preferred a more lax role as a parent, but it was in reaction to how her own parents raised her.

4. Talk about the ways you each want to parent your children and your expectations of one another as coparents.

5. Write up a clear set of guidelines for parenting. List the parenting behaviors you do not want to demonstrate as well as the ones you feel will be most beneficial to your child. Be sure to compare notes!

6. You do not have to reinvent the wheel. There are many resources for finding information on raising children. Try your local library, your children's school, and your local social services department. Parenting can be a joyous experience if you set limits for your child and yourself. Good parenting can create a happy and satisfying experience for everyone.

Chapter 21

The Power of Family

_____

A FAMILY'S STORY: *It's Been a Wild Ride!*

Steve, forty-eight, his wife Melissa, forty-five, and their two teenage children came to therapy in early April. They reported that their seventeen-year-old-daughter, Ashley, was disrupting the entire family by staying out late at night and sometimes not showing up until the next morning. Lance, their fifteen-year-old son, was talking back more and more to both parents. Steve was furious with Ashley and voiced his anger during the first session. Ashley shot back, "I'm almost eighteen and I can do whatever I want. If you don't like it, I'll just move out!" Lance sat sneering in the corner at his father and sister's fight. Melissa looked bewildered as she dejectedly complained, "I feel like I'm on a wild roller coaster ride. Is this normal or are we beyond help?"

This family was not beyond help; they were on the roller coaster ride of a normal stage of family development: emancipation of the children. Once they were reassured that this was normal, they could take the situation out of crisis mode and begin to deal with each other without the intense conflict. I began by asking Ashley when she started staying out late and she curtly replied, "October of last year." I asked what happened last October and she glared at her parents and told me to ask them. Steve spat out, "Don't tell me this is about the ski team again. We told you no and that is final!"

One way to deal with the many trials of emancipation is to come up with agreements that move both parents and children away from rigid positions. Over time, Melissa and Steve were able to voice their fears of Ashley racing down a mountain and getting injured or killed. Ashley was able to see the fear behind her parent's refusal and softened somewhat. With time her parents were able to let Ashley rejoin the ski team and Ashley agreed to take lessons with a racing coach who was an expert on speed and safety. Lance made his own agreements with his parents and seemed to drop his sarcasm simply by watching the compromise between his sister and parents.

Many families are unaware that they will go through predictable stages as the children grow and leave home. Learning that other families have experienced similar crises—a process called "normalizing the experience"—takes a lot of the shame and secrecy out of family problems. Then, and only then, can realistic agreements be made to bring about compromise instead of conflict.

THE STAGES OF FAMILY DEVELOPMENT

Jay Haley, a leader in the field of family therapy, incorporated the individual developmental model of Erik Erikson to map the stages of family development. We have modeled some of Haley's stages and added a few of our own based on our work with couples and families.

Developmental stages occur differently for different people. Some people leave home, attend college, and establish a career before they form a relationship. Others find themselves in a relationship shortly after separating from their own families; they may go through some of these stages as part of a couple. Following are some basic stages of development that most people go through either alone or in relationship.

Stage 1: The Courtship

In this stage of development, two young adults separate from their parents and begin career development and the selection of a mate. In our society, this stage is highly idealized and is often based more on physical attraction than on compatibility and partnership. This is one reason that half of all marriages end in divorce. Once the glow of "falling in love" wears thin, many couples wonder what they ever saw in the other person. If a couple can survive the end of the so-called honeymoon period, they can begin the real work of marriage and attachment.

Stage 2: Early Partnership

In this stage of life, couples begin to establish careers, achieve advanced educational goals, and establish a home life together. They both increase their separation from their parents by becoming more independent. Healthy development also sees these individuals reattaching to their parents in a more equal, adult relationship. Ties are made with new friends, with the partner's family, and with membership in a larger social community.

Stage 3: Creating a Family

This stage is associated with childbirth, adoption, rearing of small children, and the creation of blended families. For couples who do not have children, this stage might include deepening of career and creativity; passing on of knowledge to a future generation in a way that does not include having children; and expanding the coupleship by including intimate friends and family or by merging with a larger social circle such as a neighborhood, organization, or religious community. Couples usually establish their careers and economic sufficiency in this stage.

Stage 4: The Empty Nest

Much has been written in the press about the "empty nest" syndrome. Usually, the writers focus on how this period affects the mother; however, this is a stage in family development that affects each individual as well as the larger system. The *empty nest* refers to the time when all the children have reached adulthood and left their childhood home for college, marriage, or a place of their own. It is a difficult period of adjustment in which the parents must learn to treat their children as adults and the children must learn to create greater independence from their parents.

This is also a time of rediscovery for the parents. They now have the time and focus to attend to one another in a way that was not possible when the children were at home. Some marriages break down under the strain of this rediscovery. Others find it to be a wonderful period of reviving the early courtship. Many, like the boiling frog, go on with the countless details of modern life without thinking. They miss the opportunity to get out of the hot water and rediscover themselves and their partner all over again.

There are many ways for this stage of the family to go awry. If one partner has derived most of his or her identity as a parent, this period can lead to great confusion and even depression. If the parents cannot adequately let go of their children and treat them as adults, they can limit the growth of both their children and the "golden" years of their marriage. One or the other parent may choose this time to test the marriage by having an affair or creating some other breach of trust. If the children are the glue that held the marriage together, the parents may find themselves headed for divorce.

Stage 5: Loss and the Golden Years

The older we become, the closer we are to our own death and the deaths of our loved ones. We also begin to lose our physical youth: Our eyesight fails and our general health and energy slowly diminish. These are each significant losses. How do we face these times in a manner that brings us peace and enjoyment of our golden years?

Now that you have the time, follow your bliss. Is there some dream you have been privately nurturing all your life? Is there some place you have always wanted to visit? Some language, sport, hobby, or vocation you have always wanted to learn? It is never too late to pursue a dream. The advice columnist known as Dear Abby once received a letter from a woman who said, "I'm forty-three now, and I'll be fifty when I finish medical school." Abby challenged her, asking how old she would be in seven years if she did not go to medical school.

Take care of your body and mind. There is no time when it is more vital to eat healthfully, work out, and look for the good things in life. Try not to become isolated. Stay involved or become more involved in the larger community. Spend some of this time with children, some with young adults, and some with your peers. Increase your giving nature. Reach out and be helpful to others. Make peace with the mystery of death. Accepting our death allows us to be more available to life. Death is only a tragedy for those who have not truly lived.

BARRY AND MORGAN'S STORY: *Family Patterns*

Barry and Morgan were having another fight about their nineteen-year-old son, Kevin. Morgan is a forty-one-year-old realtor and appeared to be depressed at our initial meeting. Barry, aged forty-five, is a family physician and outgoing and witty. Morgan began to cry as she described her son's increased drinking and drug use. Barry simply laughed and said it was no big deal, Kevin would grow out of it. "Like your dad grew out of it!" Morgan snapped. It was time to build a structure within which this couple could have this conversation without conflict. One such structure is a family genogram. A genogram is a visual chart extending back at least two generations in a person's family (McGoldrick and

Gerson, 1985). It is a way to discover family patterns un-knowingly passed down from generation to generation.

Morgan and Barry began to create their genogram and watch as the other described his or her relationships to parents, siblings, and children. Barry talked about his father's alcoholism, which did not bother him because he had very little to do with his father. His sister, on the other hand, was very close to their father and took care of him when he went on a bender. Barry reported that his relationship with his mother was extremely close, as was his relationship with his daughter, Brandy. We charted these relationships and attributes on the genogram and a pattern began to emerge. Barry could see how he was isolated from his father and his son, both of whom were alcoholics. And he saw that he was, perhaps, too close to his daughter at his son's and wife's expense (see diagram on page 177).

Morgan noted a thread of depression that ran through her family and she worried about her daughter's and son's potential to inherit this. She also noted that her relationship with her mother was as contentious as her relationship with her daughter was. Barry and Morgan began to see the patterns that were operating under and thwarting their attempts to have a healthy family. They each saw how some of their parenting styles were not individual choices but generational habits—now they could decide what worked for them individually.

Every family has patterns that are passed from generation to generation. Some of these patterns are wonderful rituals of growth and renewal for the next generation. Sometimes these patterns can be destructive, especially when they occur without the knowledge of their origins. Barry was isolated and in denial about drinking because it was a family pattern. He needed to discover whether Barry, the individual, was as indifferent and distant as he had learned to be as a child. Morgan was in a constant battle with her mother who suffered from

BARRY AND MORGAN'S GENOGRAM

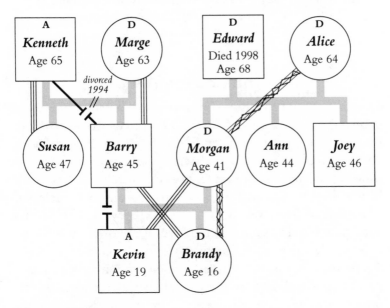

Genogram Key

A	Alcoholism
D	Depression
═══	Connected Relationship
─┤├─	Disconnected Relationship
⨳⨳⨳	Conflicted Relationship

deep bouts of depression. Morgan carried this battle into her mother-daughter relationship with Brandy. She could see from the genogram how her current relationships were battle-grounds for ancient family wars and habits.

Mark Twain once remarked that habits need to be coaxed down the stairs one step at a time. Why coax them at all? Habits are merely ingrained patterns of learned behavior. They may have little or nothing to do with who we really are or what we deeply desire. It is in our best interest to study our habitual ways of being, particularly those passed down generationally. Once we are aware of their origin and effect, we can decide whether they are patterns that we want to model in our own families.

YOUR GENOGRAM

Use Barry and Morgan's example to create your own genogram. If you are in relationship, encourage your partner to do the same. Be sure to include strengths, careers, patterns of child rearing, any addictive behaviors, the state of the relationships (connected, disconnected, or overly involved), deaths and births, divorces and marriages, affairs, and any other relevant information. The key we used in Barry and Morgan's genogram is only a suggestion. Be creative with whatever symbols you decide to use to represent traits of your family.

The next step is to share your genogram with your partner or a close friend. Explain the genogram and any patterns you notice. Encourage your partner or friend to ask questions. Sometimes new patterns emerge from questioning by an outsider. When you have completed your explanation and added any other patterns, step back and take a look at your family genogram.

YOUR FAMILY SPELL

Imagine a wizard or witch cast a damaging spell on your entire family. It is a spell cast centuries ago that is carried on from one generation to the next. Maybe the spell is depression or shame. Maybe it is abandonment or addiction. In Barry and Morgan's genogram, the spell is depression, alcoholism, and denial. Take a long look at your genogram. If you were to name a spell, what would it be?

Now that you have a name for the spell of your family, make a commitment in front of your partner or friend to break this spell and release your family from its grasp. Name some concrete steps you are willing to take to break this spell. For example, if your spell contains some kind of addiction, make a commitment to understand how this works in your life and how you can make sure not to pass this addiction along to your own children.

In Morgan's case, she committed to learn more about depression and how it affected her personally as well as her family. She began talking to her children about the family spell she had discovered, so they could make informed decisions about their own roles within the family. Barry decided to break the spell of denial, so often present in alcoholic families, and create a relationship with his son that was intimate and honest. What are you committed to change within your family?

A FAMILY'S STORY: *Honesty Is the Best Policy*

Patrick and Kim attended family counseling with their eldest son, Connor. The parents were frustrated with their son's withdrawal from the family. He did not want to go with the family on summer vacation or any weekend trips they had planned. Patrick felt hurt by Connor's insensitivity and increasing need to be alone. "I know something is bothering him. I can see it in his eyes, but he won't say a word to us," complained the father. Connor sat sullenly in the far corner, eyes focused on the patterned carpet at his feet.

"I always taught him honesty is the best policy," remarked Patrick. "If he is hiding something, then that is being dishonest and I will not have it!" It seemed it would take some time before Connor would find his voice in the family. We chose to see him individually for a session and he opened slightly at my questions. At his session he was asked how he felt about his father and he replied that he loved him very much. "But I know I'm letting him down and the truth would kill him," Connor whispered.

Many weeks into therapy, Connor and his father had built enough trust that Connor came out with his secret. "Dad," he spoke softly with tears in his eyes. "Dad, I'm gay." His father was visibly stunned by this news. After a few moments, he replied, "No you're not, Son, you're confused that's all." Connor repeated his truth several times and each time Patrick made excuses. I interrupted, "Patrick, Connor is being honest right now." Patrick sat quietly and began to understand that his son was simply telling his truth and being honest.

Patrick returned to therapy and after a time came to understand that Connor was not going to fulfill his father's dreams and expectations. Both father and son learned that disappointment is a natural part of forming relationships. It would take some time and a lot of talking, but the two men began to re-form a relationship based on the truth about each of them. Connor was able to see his father's shortcomings and accept them as he had gradually been accepted by his father.

This kind of mutual acceptance changed the way both men acted in their respective worlds. Patrick learned tolerance for people different from himself, people he may not agree with. Connor learned he could trust his father and began to trust himself more as well. He felt able to defend himself against the many prejudices he would face throughout his life, knowing that his own parents supported him.

One of the most difficult issues for family members is tolerance, or the acceptance of natural differences that arise. Some parents demand conformity and stifle the natural growth of their children. It is the task of healthy adolescents to question their parents' values and morals and decide which ones to keep and which to set aside. The best gift parents can give their children is the freedom to become the men and women they are.

Conclusion

At the beginning of this book we described a frog that was placed in water that was initially warm and relaxing. The only way to lull it into a false sense of security was to raise the temperature slowly so that it would not recognize the danger. We also might find ourselves in situations that initially feel comfortable: a new job, a new relationship, moving to another town. If we are lucky, they will be healthy transitions for us. But sometimes the new job, new relationship, or new hometown will begin to sour so slowly that we may not recognize that we are colluding with danger. Soon, what we are thinking does not align with what we are feeling or how we are behaving. Our quality of life begins to suffer on many fronts.

The nature of the water is different for all of us. Just as the frog didn't notice the increasing water temperature, we often miss the subtle changes in our own lives. The temperature of the water surrounding the frog increased, one degree at a time, until it boiled to death. In much the same way, the stresses and pressures of our lives oftentimes increases incrementally until we reach our boiling point.

You may have been able to see yourself in some of these stories. The stories were created from the kinds of real-life issues that we saw in our clients, friends, and families. You might be having problems with money, relationships, career, children, information overload, diet, exercise, or negative thinking. We hope these stories have helped you clarify the source of the stresses in your life.

Chances are, you saw pieces of your life in more than one story. Based on our experiences with hundreds of clients, we believe that the components of our lives are interconnected. If you are out of balance in one area, it is common to be out of balance in other areas as well. For example, financial problems can lead to stress on the job. Relationship problems with your partner can lead to relationship problems with your children. Stress, in general, can have a serious impact on your overall health and happiness.

The interventions provided with each story were designed to help you get out of the boiling water. Although these interventions are not the only way out, we have had the privilege to witness countless successes in the lives of our clients who used them. These are not quick fixes. They are life-changing methods that are designed to help you make integral changes that will last over time. The techniques may appear simple, yet they are not always easy and will require commitment on your part. We believe that by incorporating these techniques into your daily routine, you can turn down the heat on your own life. By getting out and staying out of hot water, the quality of your life can and will improve—one degree at a time.

Bibliography

Beck, Aaron. *Love Is Never Enough.* New York: Harper & Row, 1988

Benson, Herbert. *The Relaxation Response.* New York: William Morrow & Company, 1975

Bolton, Robert. *People Skills.* Englewood Cliffs, N.J.: Prentice-Hall, Inc., 1979

Bower, Sharon, and Gordon H. Bower. *Asserting Yourself.* New York: Addison-Wesley Publishing Company, 1991

Burns, David. *The Feeling Good Handbook.* New York: Penguin Books, 1989

Clason, George. *The Richest Man in Babylon.* New York: Penguin Books, 1955

Covey, Stephen. *The 7 Habits of Highly Effective People.* New York: Simon & Schuster, Inc., 1989

Dass, Ram, and Paul Gorman. *How Can I Help?* New York: Alfred A. Knopf, Inc., 1985

Davis, Martha, Elizabeth Robbins Eshelman, and Matthew McKay. 1996. *The Relaxation & Stress Reduction Workbook.* 4th ed. Oakland, CA: New Harbinger Publications, Inc., 1996

Gerber, Michael. *The E-Myth.* New York: HarperBusiness, 1995

Gordon, Thomas. *P.E. T.: Parent Effectiveness Training.* New York: Plume, 1970

Haas, Robert. *Eat to Win.* New York, Rawson Associates, 1983

Haley, Jay. *Problem-Solving Therapy.* San Francisco: Jossey-Bass, Inc. Publishers, 1987

Harp, David. *The Three Minute Meditator.* San Francisco: mind's I press, 1987

Hauri, Peter, and Shirley Linde. *No More Sleepless Nights.* New York: John Wiley and Sons, Inc., 1990

Heider, John. *The Tao of Leadership.* New York: Bantam Books, 1990

Hendrix, Harville. *Getting the Love You Want.* New York: Harper & Row Publishers, 1990

Jacobs, Gregg. *Say Goodnight to Insomnia.* New York: Henry Holt and Company, 1998

Kabat-Zinn, Jon. *Full Catastrophe Living.* New York: Bantam Doubleday Dell Publishing Group, Inc., 1990

Kaplan, Louis. *Adolescence: The Farewell to Childhood.* New York: Simon & Schuster, Inc., 1984

Kiyosaki, Robert, and Sharon Lechter. *Rich Dad, Poor Dad.* Paradise Valley, AZ: TechPress, Inc., 1997

Lerner, Harriet. *The Dance of Anger.* New York: HarperCollins Publishers, 1989

Levine, Stephen. *Who Dies?* New York: Bantam Doubleday Dell Publishing Group, Inc., 1982

McGoldrick, Monica, and Randy Gerson. *Genograms in Family Assessment.* New York: Norton & Company, 1985

Minuchin, Salvador. *Family Healing.* New York: Simon & Schuster, Inc., 1993

Norden, Michael. *Beyond Prozac.* New York: HarperCollins Publishers, 1995

Ornstein, Robert E., and David Sobel. *Healthy Pleasures.* New York: Addison-Wesley Publishing Company, Inc., 1989

Parker Albright, Peter, and Bets, eds. *Mind, Body and Spirit.* New York: Vail-Ballou Press, 1980

Prochaska, James, et al. *Changing for Good*. New York: Avon Books, 1994

Rogers, Carl. *On Becoming a Person*. Boston: Houghton Mifflin Company, 1961

Sears, Barry. *The Zone*. New York: ReganBooks, 1995

Senge, Peter. *The Fifth Discipline*. New York: Doubleday Currency, 1990

Shulman, Lawrence. *The Skills of Helping*. Itasca, IL: F. E. Peacock Publishers, Inc., 1992

Treacy, Michael, and Fred Wiersema. *The Discipline of Market Leaders*. New York: Addison-Wesley Publishing Company, 1995

Trout, Jack. *The New Positioning*. New York: McGraw-Hill, 1996

Weil, Andrew. *Spontaneous Healing*. New York: Alfred A. Knopf, Inc., 1986

Winfrey, Oprah, and Bob Greene. *Make the Connection*. New York: Hyperion Books, 1996

ABOUT THE AUTHORS

Shauna Ries, L.C.S.W., is a family clinician in private practice in Boulder, Colorado. She specializes in domestic violence, sexual abuse issues, and developmental issues, employing preventative therapies and interventions with individuals, couples, and families. She is a cofounder of the International Institute of Health and Wellness. Born in Sandusky, Ohio, in 1959, she received her B.A. in psychology from Union Institute, a master of social work degree from the University of Denver, and a postgraduate training degree in family therapy from the Family Therapy Training Center in Denver, Colorado. Her son, Michael Herrick, is a United States Tennis Association–ranked player, residing in Amherst, Ohio. Her passions include her family and friends, her horse Shanti, skiing, hiking, and living in the foothills of Boulder, Colorado.

Genna Murphy, L.P.C., is a licensed professional counselor with a private practice in Boulder, Colorado. She specializes in the treatment of anxiety, depression, and eating disorders in young adults. She is a cofounder of the International Institute of Health and Wellness. Born in Bellbrook, Ohio, in 1957, she received her B.A. from Wittenberg University in Springfield, Ohio; an M.A. from the University of Colorado in community development; and an M.A. from Boulder Graduate School in theoretical psychology. She completed postgraduate trainings in Gestalt therapy and Hakomi therapy. She is an accomplished musician, singer, and songwriter and an avid skier and hiker.

About the International Institute for Health and Wellness in Boulder, Colorado: Our mission is to facilitate individual, family, and community growth through innovative approaches that teach people how to develop and maintain healthy lifestyles. We offer various seminars for the public and private sectors, as well as a unique licensee program that allows other practitioners to offer our seminars in their areas to help build and maintain their current practices. For information about our licensee program or to attend a training in your area, please visit our website at www.iihw.com or call toll free, 1-877-BOULDER or 303-443-7930, or fax us at 303-444-7990.

BAKER & TAYLOR